**Airdrie 1909-2009**

*Celebrating 100 Years of History, Community and Opportunity*

**ANNA M. REBUS**

The information contained in this publication is accurate to the best of the author's and the Airdrie Centennial Committee's knowledge as of January 2009.

Cover/interior design by Jeffrey M. Cummings, K-tizo Graphic Design

Copy editor - Frances Purslow

Front cover photo courtesy Heloise (Van Sickle) Lorimer. Photo identified in the Van Sickle family album as "Frank, Fred and I (Lafe Van Sickle) doing a trick that the Trinity (Ontario) boys can't do." It is believed the three men are celebrating after striking water!

Back cover photo courtesy Tara Richards, City of Airdrie. Gymnasts from Airdrie Edge Gymnastics - Hailey Macaig, Colton Smith and Corissa Boychuk celebrating Airdrie's centennial at Genesis Place.

Printed in 2009 by
Rhino Print Solutions – Calgary, Alberta, Canada

ISBN 978-0-9811708-0-0

# Dedication

*This book is dedicated to all residents of Airdrie,*
*past and present, who have helped to shape 100 years of history,*
*and to those people that will help create its future.*

*sponsors*

The Airdrie Centennial Committee gratefully acknowledges the generosity of the sponsors who helped make this book possible.

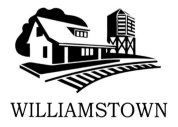

# author's note

The Airdrie centennial book is truly a celebration of 100 years of Airdrie's history. Stories, pictures, and information reveal Airdrie's pioneer roots, its emergence as a vibrant city, and the exciting future that lies ahead.

The intent of this book is to inspire readers to want to discover more of Airdrie's stories for themselves. Readers are encouraged to refer to the Further Reading section at the back of the book for additional books, articles, and websites on Airdrie and surrounding area.

The Airdrie centennial book was written using the principles of heritage interpretation as developed in the seminal book by Freeman Tilden *Interpreting Our Heritage* (1957). The writings of Dr. Sam Ham (University of Idaho) on thematic interpretation further supported this project. Each page of the book reads as its own interpretive panel.

This book is structured around a theme statement developed by the 20-member, volunteer-based Airdrie Centennial Committee. This committee worked many hours and attended many meetings to develop a theme statement that would help shape messages presented in all centennial projects. Asked to describe Airdrie, the area, and the significance of the centennial, the committee came up with words like friendly, community, pioneer, Chinooks, legacy, pride, celebration and history. From these words grew the theme statement:

*In a landscape shaped by Chinook winds and Nose Creek, a city celebrates 100 years of history built on a pioneer spirit, community pride and opportunity for the future.*

The theme statement divides the book into three parts:

- Part One explores Airdrie's pioneer spirit—highlighting Airdrie's growth and development from the determination of the early settlers to the entrepreneurs of the modern age—told as it occurred through the decades.
- Part Two celebrates Airdrie's community pride—featuring some of the people, places and events that have helped create a deep sense of community.
- Part Three imagines where Airdrie is headed in the future—exploring issues of opportunity, growth and sustainability.

In addition to this book, the Airdrie Centennial Committee created a "research binder," containing the raw research associated with the book project. Members of the community can access the binder by contacting the City of Airdrie.

# acknowledgements

The Airdrie centennial book is special because it is the result of extensive consultations with community members and contributions from them. Hundreds of people helped make this book possible. Their diligence in the pursuit of collecting and compiling details from Airdrie's past is gratefully acknowledged.

Members of the Airdrie Centennial History Committee worked tirelessly to trace local sources for pictures and stories. Thanks to committee members Sharon Bilben, Pat Jeffray, Glen Hutchings, Elaine McCracken, Dan McKinnon and Dan Melody.

The City of Airdrie staff provided leadership and direction. A special thank you to Glenda Neufeld for her encouragement, patience, laughter and diplomatic skills. Anneli Waller helped keep us organized and everything running smoothly. Tara Richards went above and beyond to track down photographs that would help tell Airdrie's story.

Thanks to Laurie Harvey and Mary Hickley at the Nose Creek Valley Museum for access to photos, archives and displays. And thanks to the unofficial 2 pm coffee club at the museum for cookies and conversation.

Community groups and clubs were asked to contribute write-ups for the book. Thank you to all those groups that took the time to send in stories and photographs; the section in the book on local clubs is a result of their efforts.

Many individuals also contributed pictures: special thanks are extended to Heloise Lorimer, Lilly Jensen and Marilyn McCall for access to, and use of, their excellent photo collections. Over tea, their stories and reminiscences helped these pictures, and Airdrie's history, come to life. Nathan Anderson and the Airdrie City View generously provided access to photographic archives.

Pat Molesky-Brar and Susan Kooyman at the Glenbow Library and Archives were very helpful in sourcing historical files and information. Thank you also to the Airdrie Public Library, and the newspaper archives made available from the *Airdrie Echo*. Rona McLeod and Sylvia Harnden at Heritage Park Historical Village provided access to park buildings, displays and archives. AirdrieLIFE Magazine is also thanked for allowing access to their photo archives.

A long-distance thank you must go out to Judi Francis with the South Australian Department for Environment and Heritage. Her creative approach to heritage interpretation, storytelling and design, provided great inspiration for this project.

Fran Purslow and Carol Koopmans are thanked for their fine editing skills, constructive comments and incredible efficiency!

Jeff Cummings is thanked for his enthusiasm, creativity and dedication to this project. His ability to weave together text and images has resulted in a beautiful finished product.

It has been a privilege to get to know the history, people and places that make Airdrie such an exceptional place to live.

This project was funded in part by the Alberta Historical Resources Foundation.

Airdrie Centennial History Committee: Back row (L-R) Glen Hutchings, Glenda Neufeld, Dan McKinnon
Front row (L-R) Sharon Bilben, Pat Jeffray, Anna Rebus, Elaine McCracken, (missing Dan Melody)

# table of contents

## part one: pioneer spirit

### The early pioneer spirit 1909-1958

### The modern pioneer spirit 1959-2009

# part two: community pride

## The people make the city

## Familiar, favourite and unforgettable places

## Where the streets (and communities, parks and schools!) have historic names

## Clubs, organizations and societies

# part three: opportunity for the future

PRIME MINISTER . PREMIER MINISTRE

I am pleased to extend my sincere congratulations to all the readers of the Centennial Book, and to everyone celebrating Airdrie's 100th anniversary.

This milestone offers an ideal opportunity to reflect upon the history of your community. In 1890, the waters of Nose Creek made this spot an ideal reststop for the Calgary and Edmonton Railway and, ever since, Airdrie has flourished. Incorporated as a village in 1909, Airdrie has played a significant role in the growth of central Alberta, and can look to its future with great optimism. With its smalltown qualities and access to Calgary, Airdrie will undoubtedly continue to be a vibrant and thriving community.

I am sure that this Centennial Book will be enjoyed by all who read it, and I join you in giving special thanks to all those who have had a hand in the commemoration of this special occasion: you may be certain that your efforts and community spirit are truly appreciated.

On behalf of the Government of Canada, please accept my best wishes for a memorable celebration, and for every future success.

The Rt. Hon. Stephen Harper, P.C., M.P.

*OTTAWA*
*2009*

## Message from Honourable Ed Stelmach
## Premier of Alberta

On behalf of the Government of Alberta, it is my pleasure to congratulate the City of Airdrie and all its residents on its 100th anniversary.

Every village, town and city in Alberta has a unique story to tell – stories of the land, of the people and of the places. History preservation celebrates and documents the past and also helps to educate future generations, which greatly contributes to Albertans' quality of life.

What started as a small railway community in the early 1900s, Airdrie has transformed into a vibrant and industrious city. With citizens famous for their western hospitality, and a number of attractions like beautiful Nose Creek Park, Airdrie is a city that everyone should experience.

I want to give special thanks to the Airdrie Centennial Committee, as well as everyone else involved in making this historical publication possible. Your dedication to your city and its history is certainly commendable.

Happy Anniversary!

Ed Stelmach

*Ed Stelmach*

*September 2009*

HOUSE OF COMMONS
CHAMBRE DES COMMUNES

# Message from Blake Richards
## Member of Parliament
## Wild Rose

September 2009

On behalf of the Government of Canada and as your Parliamentary representative, it is my privilege to extend a warm congratulations and best wishes to the City of Airdrie and its residents as we celebrate our centennial.

For 100 years Airdrie has been transforming from a little railroad town to a large, up-and-coming city centre that embraces both business and community. Throughout these changes it has not lost its small-town charm, and the warmth and friendliness of its people shines as brightly as our annual Festival of Lights. It is but one of the reasons why I am proud to call Airdrie home.

To the Airdrie Centennial Committee, I commend you for recognizing the importance of this occasion and taking the time to document it as an important part of our history. I know it is but one of the many milestones this wonderful city will be achieving throughout the years to come. For a city like Airdrie, the sky is the limit.

Happy 100th Birthday Airdrie! As we remember our past, we will celebrate our future!

Sincerely,

Blake Richards, M.P.
Wild Rose

XVI | Airdrie Centennial

**Rob Anderson, MLA**
Airdrie – Chestermere
Parliamentary Assistant to the Solicitor General &
Minister of Public Security

September 2009

Happy Birthday Airdrie!

In 2009, the City of Airdrie celebrates its 100th birthday. I am hounoured as the Member of the Legislative Assembly for the Constituency of Airdrie – Chestermere to extend congratulations to the City of Airdrie on this very special occasion - its centennial year.

The community of Airdrie was incorporated as a village in 1909, a town in 1974 and a city in 1985. This is a great opportunity to commemorate Airdrie's heritage and I am delighted the Airdrie Centennial Committee has undertaken the task of documenting our local history in this publication. Recognizing our past is an important part of who we are.

It is the residents who truly make communities so special and Airdrie is certainly no exception to this, from the pioneers to the present. You indeed have made Airdrie one of the best places to reside in this province. I am confident this community will continue to thrive and prosper as it moves into the next century.

So Airdrie, let the celebrations begin. Again, please accept my sincere congratulations on achieving this milestone – 100 years.

Rob Anderson, MLA

CITY of
AIRDRIE
COMMUNITY & OPPORTUNITY

September 2009

Airdrie centennial: a new era, a new celebration

Airdrie's centennial brings a significant opportunity to reflect on development throughout our history. This is a time to remember our roots, live in the moment and celebrate a brand new century.

Centennial reminds us of how our early pioneers provided us with the foundation for our vibrant community. Airdrie was first established as a railway town. Ideal farm land fashioned Airdrie into an agricultural prairie centre. The hard work of our ancestors has brought new faces and new development giving rise to the community that Airdrie is today.

Together, I invite you to celebrate and commemorate our city. Airdrie is making a name for itself. We have experienced tremendous growth in the last decade of our century, attracting consumers, tourists, families and industry. This moment in time is clearly where community and opportunity have intersected, and now Airdrie is a place where we can live, shop, work and play.

Airdrie is boldly emerging into a dynamic and energetic city. Reaching 100 years of age is an extraordinary milestone. Airdrie's centennial is a celebration of our community. Our ancestors, our residents and our future generations have provided and will continue to provide the vision to move Airdrie forward.

Airdrie has always harbored small town charm and community spirit. As we move into the future, it is this energy that will drive Airdrie towards reaching new heights and accomplishments in a new era.

I invite all residents to remember yesterday, live today and celebrate tomorrow.

Airdrie, congratulations on becoming 100 years old!

Mayor

Linda Bruce

CA. 1910

AiRDRiE ALTA

GEORGE HATT LUMBER

GLOVER McCORMACK GENERAL MERCHANTS

2008

*In a landscape shaped by Chinook winds and Nose Creek,*

*a city celebrates 100 years of history built on a pioneer spirit,*

*community pride and opportunity for the future.*

Part One

*pioneer spirit*

The pioneer spirit defined early settlement in western Canada. Homesteaders headed west in search of fertile lands for farming and new opportunities. Settlers experienced many hardships and struggles, but persevered in their quest for a better way of life.

Pioneer spirit shaped Airdrie's story. Settlers to the area relied on their own resourcefulness and hard work to create not just a place to live, but a community in which to watch their children grow.

This first section of the book explores the pioneer spirit that helped to build the village of Airdrie during its first half-century of development. Stories from each decade highlight the trials and tribulations together with the triumphs that villagers experienced in their everyday life.

early pioneer spirit
1909–1958

## THE FIRST PIONEERS
*Settling the frontier*

While Airdrie became a village in 1909, its story actually began in the 1870s. At this time, American-born trader, sheep rancher and freighter Addison McPherson became one of the first people to settle near Airdrie, in the area known today as McPherson Coulee.[1] In 1883, McPherson, along with John Coleman, began running the mail by stagecoach on the Calgary to Edmonton Trail.[2] By 1899, McPherson was operating the Black Diamond Coal Mine in Black Diamond, Alberta.[3]

Another entrepreneurial pioneer, John Dickson, arrived in the Airdrie area by 1880.[4] By 1886, he was running Dickson's Stopping House, built along the Calgary to Edmonton Trail.[5] "Stopping houses" provided weary travelers (and animals) with food and shelter. Accommodation was very basic, but better than a night in the cold outdoors. Charges varied from 50 cents to $1.50.[6] Dickson's Stopping House was noted in a North West Mounted Police report as being a day's journey north of Calgary.[7]

In 1895, Johnston Stevenson obtained title to Dickson's Stopping House (although he may have been there well before this time).[8] In addition to providing accommodation, the stopping house served as post office, makeshift church and social hub. People from all walks of life stayed there— from clergymen just passing through to North West Mounted Police officers with prisoners in handcuffs.[9]

With the building of the Calgary and Edmonton Railway in 1890–1891, the need for this stopping house began to decline. It closed in 1900.[10]

## The Riel (North-West) Rebellion Connection

During the Riel Rebellion of 1885, Johnston Stevenson took up arms against the Métis. He would suffer a wound to his lung.[11]

A North West Mounted Police detachment from Calgary would camp at McPherson Coulee on its way to engage the Cree at Frenchman's Butte, Saskatchewan. Major General T. Bland Strange recorded that experience.

*21st (April 1885) – The column marched to and camped at McPherson's Coulee. A snowstorm came on, and continued next day. The tents were frozen stiff the ropes like rods, and the pegs had to be chopped out of the frozen ground with axes.*[12]

Major General T. Bland Strange
The Story of Riel's Revolt
Canada: 1885

MAJOR GENERAL
T. BLAND STRANGE

Glenbow Archives NA-1847-2

CALGARY TO EDMONTON STAGECOACH CROSSING A MUD HOLE, CA. 1888

The Sharp Hills Stagecoach Robbery

Alberta's first (and believed to be only) stagecoach robbery occurred just south of Airdrie in the Sharp Hills on August 23, 1886.[13] Wearing masks made from a Union Jack, and brandishing guns, two bandits stole several hundred dollars from the coach driver and three passengers. No one was ever apprehended, but two known criminals, Charlie Lafferty and Jack Young, were the primary suspects. They were also suspects in the murder of "Clinker" Scott Krueger two days after the robbery.

Glenbow Archives NA-1162-9

### The Calgary to Edmonton Trail

First Nations people traveled across this vast wilderness on tracks and trails for many millennia. These trails became travel routes for early explorers, traders, missionaries and eventually homesteaders. In 1883, the Canadian Pacific Railway brought settlers to Calgary. Leaving the train, they traveled north along the Calgary to Edmonton Trail with all their worldly possessions. In the same year, the stagecoach began making its regular five-day run between these two towns.[14] While travel on the trail decreased with the arrival of the Calgary and Edmonton Railway, the trail provided the backbone for the modern road system between these two cities.

CALGARY – EDMONTON STAGECOACH ENROUTE, 1890

Glenbow Archives NA-1905-1

Between 1900 and 1903, Johnston Stevenson served as postmaster, dispensing mail from his house.[15] The post office moved into Airdrie in 1903.

DICKSON-STEVENSON STOPPING HOUSE, CA. 1890

Glenbow Archives NA-582-1

ADDISON D. McPHERSON, MAY 1928

Glenbow Archives NA-2354-6

Glenbow Archives NA-1231-1

## BUILDING OF THE CALGARY AND EDMONTON RAILWAY 1890–1891

*Laying the tracks*

Airdrie owes its existence to the building of the Calgary and Edmonton Railway.

In 1890, business partners Herbert Holt, William Mackenzie, Donald Mann and James Ross formed the Calgary and Edmonton Railway Company.[16] In July of that same year, construction began on the railway in Calgary, reaching Edmonton (Strathcona) by the following summer.[17] The future site of Airdrie made an ideal stopping point for the trains to take on water to run the steam engines. With a low alkali (salt) content, the waters of Nose Creek provided thirsty steam trains with a much needed drink.

Settlements soon began to spring up around the sidings and stations along the railway line. Airdrie's first buildings supported the upkeep of the railway and these included a station, a section house, a windmill and a water tank. Railway maintenance workers lived and worked in the section house. These workers became Airdrie's first residents.[18]

## Airdrie: The Great Name Debate!

Airdrie, Alberta, is named after the town of Airdrie, Scotland.[19] The true origin and the meaning of the word "Airdrie" is a source of great debate among the Scots. Some suggest the name comes from a Gaelic term *Ard Ruith* meaning a level height, high slope or high pasture land. Others say it comes from Arderyth, the scene of the battle in 577 AD between the armies of Aeddam, King of Kintyre, and Rydderych the Bountiful, King of Strathclyde. Still others say it comes from *Aird Righ*, Gaelic for High King.[20] Despite the debate, it is certain the name is ancient and is one of countless examples of Scottish place names found in southern Alberta.[21]

The person responsible for naming Airdrie, Alberta, and the date it was named is also up for discussion. Naming dates range from 1889 to 1893. Some say that Sir William Mackenzie named Airdrie, Alberta, in honour of his Scottish roots, while others suggest one of the many Scottish railway workers named the stopping point.

Born in Ontario in 1849 to Scottish parents, Sir William Mackenzie was considered one of Canada's great entrepreneurs during the late nineteenth and early twentieth centuries. Contracted to build the Calgary and Edmonton Railway, he also "laid the tracks" for other well-known enterprises, including the Canadian National Railway and the Toronto Transit Commission. Described by historian R.B. Fleming as "the railway king of Canada," Sir Mackenzie also undertook projects in Maine, Brazil and Europe.[22] Knighted in 1911, his empire fell into decline during the years of the First World War. He died in 1923, and is buried in Kirkfield, Ontario.[23]

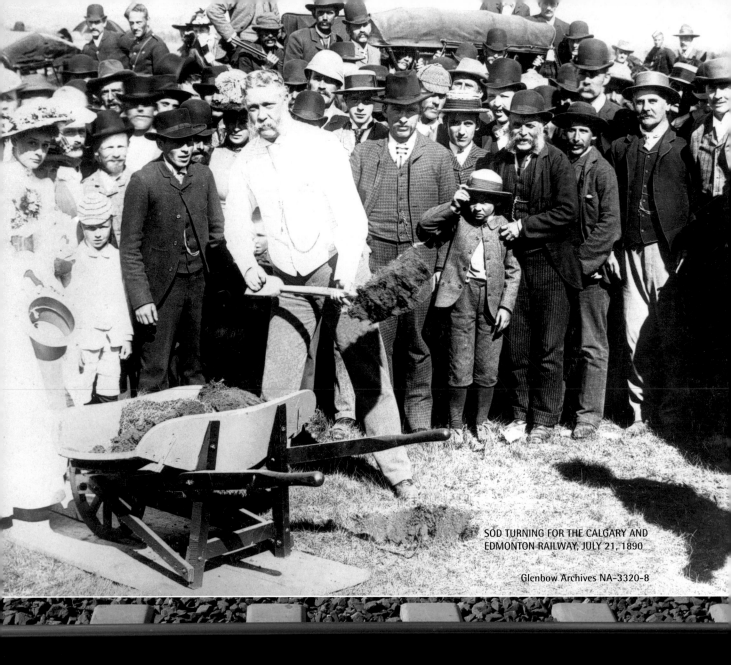

SOD TURNING FOR THE CALGARY AND
EDMONTON RAILWAY, JULY 21, 1890

Glenbow Archives NA–3320-8

## Sod turning ceremony for the Calgary and Edmonton Railway

The ceremony was performed by the Honourable Edgar Dewdney, Lieutenant-Governor of the North West Territories. It did not need much physical exertion on his part, to do this. He simply took his place between the handles of a wheelbarrow, in which a few sods had been placed; and on a given signal, he took hold of the handles, and dumped out the sods.[24]

P. Turner Bone
*When the Steel Went Through – Reminiscences of a Railroad Pioneer*
*1947*

MEMBERS OF THE CALGARY AND EDMONTON RAILWAY SURVEY TEAM – PLAYING POKER!

Glenbow Archives NA-1905-13

CONSTRUCTION WORK ON THE CALGARY AND EDMONTON RAILWAY, 1890.

Glenbow Archives NA-1905-15

## BEYOND THE RAILWAY STOP

*Roots take hold*

Firmly established by the spring of 1901, the roots for the hamlet of Airdrie had taken hold when the Province of Alberta was still a vast land called the North West Territories, District of Alberta.

Arriving in 1901, homesteaders A.E. Bowers and his brother-in-law W.H. Croxford were Airdrie's first true settlers. They constructed Airdrie's first buildings, including a barn and family homes. A.E. Bowers also built a small general store and post office on the north side of his house. Very quickly, more settlers arrived, and Airdrie soon found itself offering complete community services: a church, school, hardware store, grain elevator, restaurant, blacksmith and hotel.[25]

The railway continued to sustain the growing hamlet by transporting not only people, but grain, cattle, coal and supplies. Residents also received their mail by rail; mailbags were tossed from the train as it passed through the hamlet. A poor throw could result in residents receiving a soggy batch of mail!

VAN SICKLE FAMILY HOME, EARLY 1900s

Glenbow Archives NA-3765-4

CROXFORD FAMILY HOME, EARLY 1900s

# Horses, hay bales and harvests

At the same time the hamlet of Airdrie began to take shape, homesteaders staked their land claims to settle the surrounding area. Converting open prairie to productive farm land demanded back-breaking labour. Heavy workhorses pulled plows that broke the prairie grassland. Men walked behind these plows to till the soil and break up the sod for planting. The conversion of open prairie to farmland is the story of real horsepower at work!

Farming was often a team effort with neighbours banding together to get a job done. In times of crisis or need, friends helped friends till the land, sow seed and harvest the crops. Ranchers also used the same team approach to round up cattle for branding or dipping (to get rid of disease).

At the constant mercy of Mother Nature, farmers depended on the right mix of sun and rain for a bumper crop. An early frost, snowstorm, hailstorm, drought, grasshopper infestation or grass fire could prove disastrous.

1912—Farming for Mr. Adam Watson
8 miles west of Airdrie and about
20 miles from Calgary. He homesteaded
here just 10 years ago. I got top
wages $25 a month. In the morning
when driving the team one can see
the mountains all rosy pink the early
morning sun shining on the snow and
at evening they look a violety gray.[26]

Stanley Brooker
1977

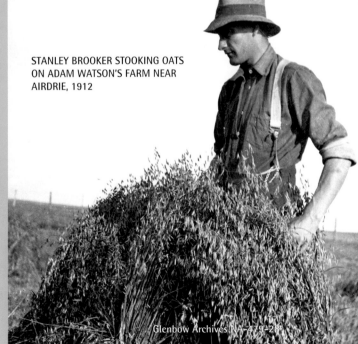

STANLEY BROOKER STOOKING OATS
ON ADAM WATSON'S FARM NEAR
AIRDRIE, 1912

Glenbow Archives NA-479-28

## A HAMLET BECOMES A VILLAGE

*Building a sense of place*

With a growing number of people, shops and homes, Airdrie had become more than a stopping point for the railway; it had become a settlement with a true sense of place.

Efforts to become registered as a village began December 23, 1908.[27] After nine months of paperwork between the provincial government and the hamlet, the Village of Airdrie was born September 10, 1909—a significant birth date and cause for celebration.[28]

Those people who had dared to homestead the land and build a hamlet now found themselves pioneers of village life. In the coming years, early settlers, including A.E. Bowers, Dr. W.F. Edwards, R.J. Hawkey, J.R. McCracken, J.E. Fletcher, L. Flett, L. Van Sickle and L. Farr, balanced home and work life with council duties.[29] Village business included decisions on building sidewalks, purchasing a fire engine, levying and collecting fees, and replacing the town pump.

AIRDRIE STREET VIEW, CA. 1907-1909

Glenbow Archives PA 3689-335

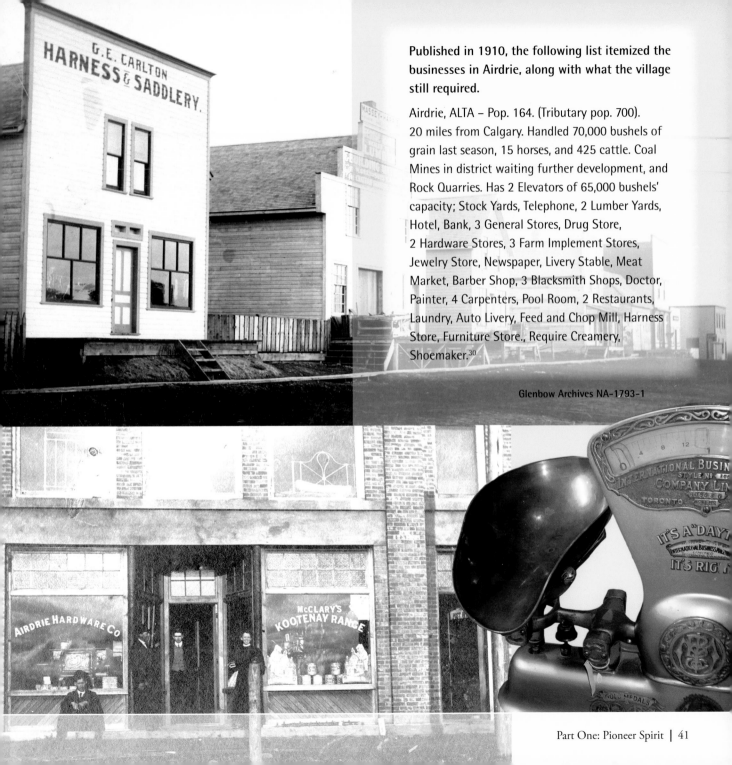

Published in 1910, the following list itemized the businesses in Airdrie, along with what the village still required.

Airdrie, ALTA – Pop. 164. (Tributary pop. 700). 20 miles from Calgary. Handled 70,000 bushels of grain last season, 15 horses, and 425 cattle. Coal Mines in district waiting further development, and Rock Quarries. Has 2 Elevators of 65,000 bushels' capacity; Stock Yards, Telephone, 2 Lumber Yards, Hotel, Bank, 3 General Stores, Drug Store, 2 Hardware Stores, 3 Farm Implement Stores, Jewelry Store, Newspaper, Livery Stable, Meat Market, Barber Shop, 3 Blacksmith Shops, Doctor, Painter, 4 Carpenters, Pool Room, 2 Restaurants, Laundry, Auto Livery, Feed and Chop Mill, Harness Store, Furniture Store., Require Creamery, Shoemaker.[30]

Glenbow Archives NA-1793-1

# Blacksmith shops
## Forging the future

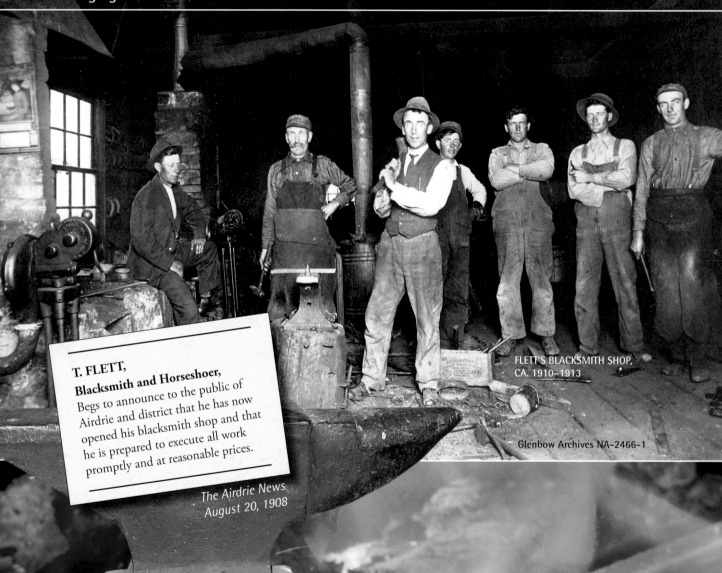

**T. FLETT,**
**Blacksmith and Horseshoer,**
Begs to announce to the public of Airdrie and district that he has now opened his blacksmith shop and that he is prepared to execute all work promptly and at reasonable prices.

*The Airdrie News,*
*August 20, 1908*

FLETT'S BLACKSMITH SHOP,
CA. 1910–1913

Glenbow Archives NA-2466-1

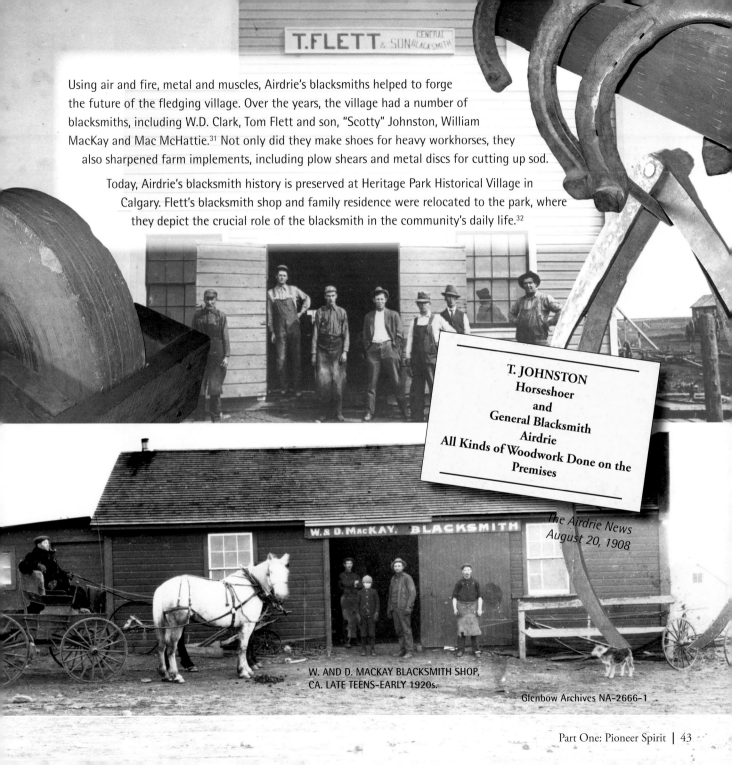

T.FLETT & SON GENERAL BLACKSMITH

Using air and fire, metal and muscles, Airdrie's blacksmiths helped to forge the future of the fledging village. Over the years, the village had a number of blacksmiths, including W.D. Clark, Tom Flett and son, "Scotty" Johnston, William MacKay and Mac McHattie.[31] Not only did they make shoes for heavy workhorses, they also sharpened farm implements, including plow shears and metal discs for cutting up sod.

Today, Airdrie's blacksmith history is preserved at Heritage Park Historical Village in Calgary. Flett's blacksmith shop and family residence were relocated to the park, where they depict the crucial role of the blacksmith in the community's daily life.[32]

T. JOHNSTON
Horseshoer
and
General Blacksmith
Airdrie
All Kinds of Woodwork Done on the
Premises

*The Airdrie News*
*August 20, 1908*

W. & D. MacKAY. BLACKSMITH

W. AND D. MACKAY BLACKSMITH SHOP,
CA. LATE TEENS-EARLY 1920s.

Glenbow Archives NA-2666-1

# Women in the village and on the farm
## The feminine touch!

A vast and mainly treeless landscape greeted early arrivals to the new village of Airdrie. Women did what they could to "soften" their somewhat desolate prairie surroundings. Spring and summer meant gardening. They planted flowers for beauty and vegetable gardens for food. Winter forced everyone indoors. "Handiwork" meant time spent making handmade quilts, knitting or crocheting clothes, and tatting beautiful lace to decorate pillowcases or use as doilies.

Women's work was never done. Women were responsible for preparing hearty meals for the family and hired help. During harvest, threshing crews traveled from farm to farm. This could mean serving meals three times a day for 20 or more people, until the harvest was finished and the crew moved to the next farm.

Some women also worked outside the home. They worked in the village as teachers, as post mistresses, as nurses and telephone operators. Women were involved with the home and school association, while the men usually sat on the school board.

In 1916, the Airdrie Branch of the Alberta Women's Institute was established. For a 25¢ membership, women learned about systematic housekeeping, war-time economy, country sanitation and bread-making.[33] Members also worked to raise funds for community projects, including playground equipment for the school and upkeep of the cemetery. In 1925, Famous Five member Nellie McClung spoke to the Airdrie Women's Institute about her life and books.[34] The Institute was later replaced by the Airdrie Women's Community Club.

*When we first came to Airdrie, there wasn't a tree in sight!*
Margaret (Carlson) Fowler
2007

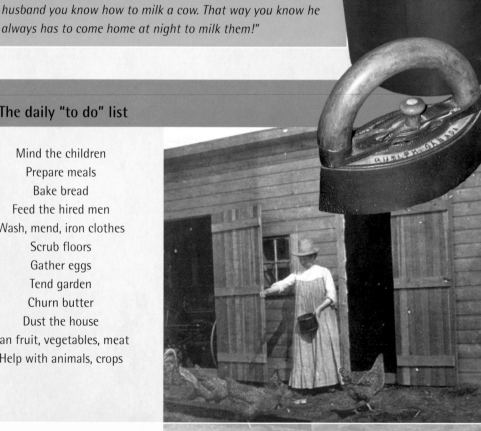

MARGIE REID, JANUARY 24, 1937

## Me, milk a cow? What?!

Brides-to-be are always given advice before the big day. Perhaps the best advice local farm wives received was: *"Never tell your husband you know how to milk a cow. That way you know he always has to come home at night to milk them!"*

## The daily "to do" list

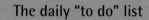

Mind the children
Prepare meals
Bake bread
Feed the hired men
Wash, mend, iron clothes
Scrub floors
Gather eggs
Tend garden
Churn butter
Dust the house
Can fruit, vegetables, meat
Help with animals, crops

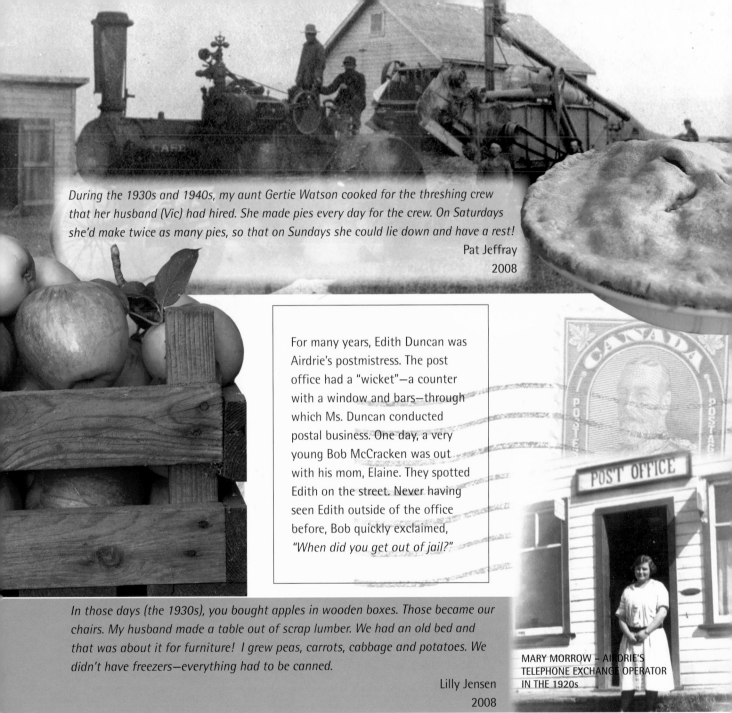

During the 1930s and 1940s, my aunt Gertie Watson cooked for the threshing crew that her husband (Vic) had hired. She made pies every day for the crew. On Saturdays she'd make twice as many pies, so that on Sundays she could lie down and have a rest!

Pat Jeffray
2008

For many years, Edith Duncan was Airdrie's postmistress. The post office had a "wicket"—a counter with a window and bars—through which Ms. Duncan conducted postal business. One day, a very young Bob McCracken was out with his mom, Elaine. They spotted Edith on the street. Never having seen Edith outside of the office before, Bob quickly exclaimed, *"When did you get out of jail?"*

In those days (the 1930s), you bought apples in wooden boxes. Those became our chairs. My husband made a table out of scrap lumber. We had an old bed and that was about it for furniture! I grew peas, carrots, cabbage and potatoes. We didn't have freezers—everything had to be canned.

Lilly Jensen
2008

MARY MORROW – AIRDRIE'S TELEPHONE EXCHANGE OPERATOR IN THE 1920s

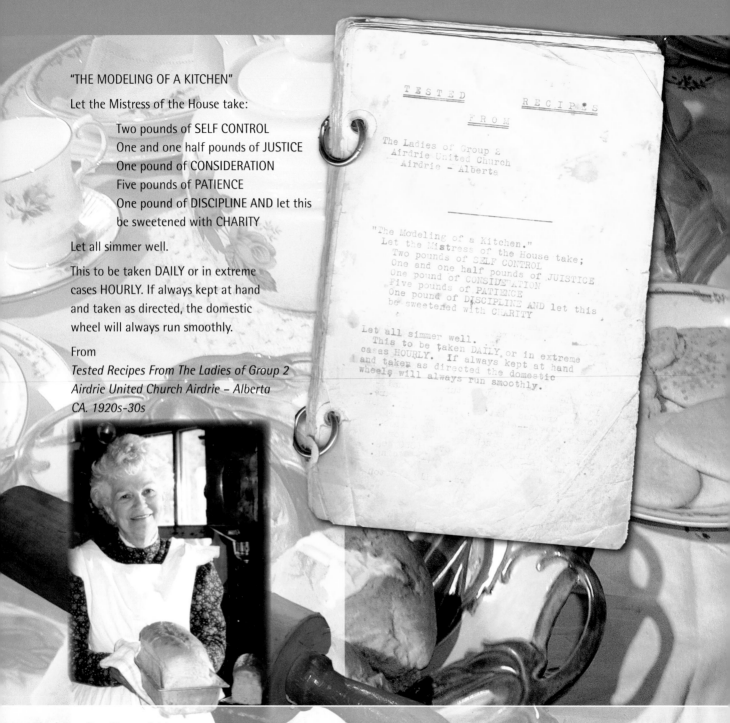

## "THE MODELING OF A KITCHEN"

Let the Mistress of the House take:

> Two pounds of SELF CONTROL
> One and one half pounds of JUSTICE
> One pound of CONSIDERATION
> Five pounds of PATIENCE
> One pound of DISCIPLINE AND let this
> be sweetened with CHARITY

Let all simmer well.

This to be taken DAILY or in extreme cases HOURLY. If always kept at hand and taken as directed, the domestic wheel will always run smoothly.

From
*Tested Recipes From The Ladies of Group 2*
*Airdrie United Church Airdrie – Alberta*
*CA. 1920s-30s*

## Mrs. Adam's Prize Sponge Cake

5 egg whites     5 egg yolks
5 tbsp. cold water     1 cup sugar
1 cup cake flour     1 tsp. Cream tartar
1 tsp. each l

Put egg yolks
large mixing
double Dover
then add flou
Beat egg whit
of tartar, be
the cake. Ba
1 hour at 300

MRS. ADAM'S PRIZE SPONGE CAKE

5 egg whites
5 egg yolks
5 tablespoons cold water
1 cup sugar
1 cup cake flour
1 teaspoon cream of tartar
1 tsp each lemon and vanilla

Put egg yolks, sugar and water into a large mixing bowl
and beat with large double Dover egg beater for
10 minutes.* Then add flour and flavouring, beat well. (In
a separate bowl) beat egg whites until foamy. Add cream
of tartar, beat until dry and fold into the cake. Bake
in an ungreased pan for 1 hour at 300 degrees
(moderate heat). Invert pan and let "hang" till cool,
about 1 hour.

Thelma Allan

*A Dover egg beater was a hand-cranked beater with
metal blades.

# School days
## Golden rule days

As with most pioneer towns on the prairies, Airdrie's first school was a one-room schoolhouse. Built in 1904, the school opened with a dozen students and R.J. Hawkey as teacher.[35]

Children from all grades learned and played together. Students got to school either by walking or riding a pony, which they stabled in the schoolyard barn during the school day. On cold winter days, parents hitched up wagons and picked-up neighbour kids for the trip to and from school.

Lessons focused on "the 3 R's"— Reading, 'Riting and 'Rithmetic. Spelling bees and math competitions were part of everyday learning. Memorizing the times tables was particularly important, but there was also time for fun. The students and teacher worked hard to make the Christmas Pageant an entertaining event. Students also played games in the schoolyard.[36]

AIRDRIE'S FIRST SCHOOL, CA. 1904 WITH R.J. HAWKEY IN BACK ROW

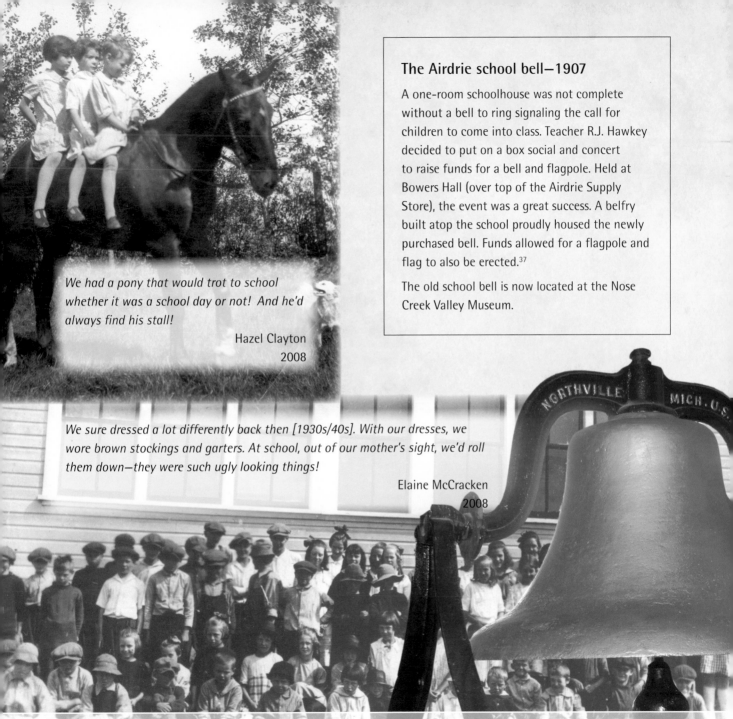

*We had a pony that would trot to school whether it was a school day or not! And he'd always find his stall!*

Hazel Clayton
2008

### The Airdrie school bell—1907

A one-room schoolhouse was not complete without a bell to ring signaling the call for children to come into class. Teacher R.J. Hawkey decided to put on a box social and concert to raise funds for a bell and flagpole. Held at Bowers Hall (over top of the Airdrie Supply Store), the event was a great success. A belfry built atop the school proudly housed the newly purchased bell. Funds allowed for a flagpole and flag to also be erected.[37]

The old school bell is now located at the Nose Creek Valley Museum.

*We sure dressed a lot differently back then [1930s/40s]. With our dresses, we wore brown stockings and garters. At school, out of our mother's sight, we'd roll them down—they were such ugly looking things!*

Elaine McCracken
2008

## WWI AND THE INFLUENZA EPIDEMIC
*The war away, the struggle at home*

Are **YOU** in this?

As Airdrie settled into village routine, two major events on the world stage would have a significant impact on daily life. World War I was declared in 1914. Several dozen young men from Airdrie and district signed up for service.[38] The same traits that had drawn these men to pioneer life—courage, grit and resilience—drew them into service. Most of these local servicemen returned home, but a few did not, including William Jones, Alexander MacArthur, Bernard Tyas and Earl Weeger.[39] Their sacrifice deeply impacted the small community.

Just as the war ended in 1918, the world faced a new danger: the Spanish Influenza epidemic. During 1918 and 1919, the flu epidemic spread across the world, killing millions. This global disaster did not leave Airdrie untouched. To minimize exposure, village council proposed strict shopping hours. Gatherings were restricted to very small groups. Caution necessitated the temporary closure of the church. Despite these measures, the flu spread throughout the village and district. The local doctor, Dr. Edwards, could not possibly attend to all the sick himself. At the height of the outbreak, the Old Hotel became a makeshift hospital with emergency supplies provided by the Red Cross.

During this crisis, the entire village came together with their usual degree of determination. Many people pitched in by making meals, cleaning rooms, doing laundry and helping with the sick. Thanks to the tireless efforts of Dr. Edwards, the nursing skills of Margaret Kinniburgh and the help of countless village members, only four Airdrie residents died from the flu. They are buried in the Airdrie Cemetery.[40]

# EPIDEMIC INFLUENZA (SPANISH)

## This Disease is Highly Communicable.
## It May Develop Into a Severe Pneumonia.

There is no medicine which will prevent it.

Keep away from public meetings, theatres and other places where crowds are assembled.

Keep the mouth and nose covered while coughing or sneezing.

When a member of the household becomes ill, place him in a room by himself.

The room should be warm, but well ventilated.

The attendant should put on a mask before entering the room of those ill of the disease.

### TO MAKE A MASK

Take a piece of ordinary cheesecloth 8 x 16 inches, fold it to make it 8 x 8 inches. Next fold this to make it 8 x 4 inches. Tie cords about 10 inches long at each corner. Apply over mouth and nose as shown in the picture.

## ISSUED BY THE PROVINCIAL BOARD OF HEALTH

Glenbow Archives NA-4548-5

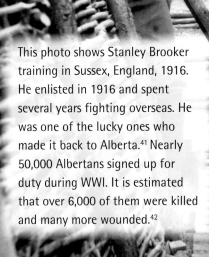

This photo shows Stanley Brooker training in Sussex, England, 1916. He enlisted in 1916 and spent several years fighting overseas. He was one of the lucky ones who made it back to Alberta.[41] Nearly 50,000 Albertans signed up for duty during WWI. It is estimated that over 6,000 of them were killed and many more wounded.[42]

Glenbow Archives NA-479-10

## THE 1920s
*The road to recovery*

As the people of Airdrie recovered physically and emotionally from the effects of war and influenza, they once again turned their energies to building their village.

Road building projects increased during the 1920s and 1930s. The rolling prairie landscape proved a challenge in the early days of road building. Filling gullies, draining sloughs, laying gravel and building bridges were all in a day's work. Road crews used horse teams to haul dirt and gravel. It was tough and sometimes dangerous work, but farmers were keen to get on a road crew, as the wages helped pay their farm taxes.[43] These back-breaking efforts made travel much easier with each completed project.

The year 1923 marked the formation of the Alberta Wheat Pool.[44] This grain marketing cooperative quickly took hold in Airdrie and area. By 1929, Airdrie had its first Pool grain elevator. In the decades to follow, the elevator was "twinned" and additions built, greatly increasing bushel capacity.

In 1928, the "lights went on" in Airdrie. The village council granted Calgary Power Ltd. the contract to supply Airdrie with lights and power.[45]

A MULE TEAM FROM THE JACKSON CONSTRUCTION COMPANY WORKING ON ROAD CONSTRUCTION IN THE AIRDRIE AREA.

Glenbow Archives NA-2579-11

CAR AUCTION, EARLY 1930s

WORKING ON AN IRRIGATION DITCH, EARLY 1900s

# *Electricity comes to Airdrie*

## We've got the power!

Farmers and ranchers generated their own electricity in the early 1900s. Old wind-chargers, water pumps and batteries document a tradition of self-reliance and improvisation. Wind-chargers stood tall on a tripod, harnessing southern Alberta's prairie winds. With each turn of the charger blades, batteries stored electricity for future use. Generators, lanterns and candles provided back-up on windless days.

In 1926, Calgary Power Ltd. began running electricity lines north toward Olds and beyond. A substation was built just southwest of Airdrie, and in 1928, the village "got the power".[46] This had a dramatic impact on the community, changing the way in which people lived, worked and played.

ORVILLA KININMONTH
IRONING QUILT PATCHES

While Airdrie enjoyed the benefits of being on the electricity grid, it would take nearly 20 years before area farms fully embraced this convenience. This is likely due to the fact that the 1930s and 1940s were difficult times for farmers, who were just recovering from the effects of the depression when they were faced with rationing during WWII. Farmers had also been self-sufficient for so long, it might have been a case of "if it isn't broken, don't fix it"!

Formed in 1948, the West Airdrie Rural Electrification Association investigated bringing electricity to area farms under a scheme run by Calgary Power Ltd. (then called Farm Electric Services Ltd).[47] By the early 1950s, many farms were on the grid. Access to reliable electricity changed farming life, just as it had changed village life. Families could run power tools, milking machines, outdoor lights, water pumps, kitchen gadgets and more. A new era in farming had begun.

In the 1930s, Calgary Power Ltd. hit the road with a traveling "Modern All-Electric Kitchen". It showcased the benefits of electricity in the home. Airdrie was its first stop.[48] In 1981, Calgary Power Ltd. changed its name to TransAlta Utilities Corporation.[49]

*Before 1948, we had a wind-charger. The batteries were stored in the basement and had 32 volts of power. You could only iron when it was windy!*

Jim and Jessie Bussey
2007

# *We made our own fun*

If you ask an Airdrie old-timer what he or she did for fun, the response is often, "We worked and did chores!" Delve a little deeper and you discover it wasn't all work and no play. Everyone made their own fun.

Children enjoyed activities such as baseball, swimming and horseback riding during the summer, and skating and playing hockey during the winter. Hide-and-seek was a year-round favourite, as was "giant strides," which involved a tall post with chains attached to it with handles. Kids would grab onto the handles and run like the wind in circles. They got going so fast they almost flew! Toys included small wagons, tricycles and dolls. And a special treat was a trip to the store to buy penny candy.

During Halloween, kids played tricks in the village. Tipping over outhouses was especially popular!

Fun for the adults often meant going to dances or hosting dinners. For the more sporting types, hockey in winter and baseball in summer provided both recreation and entertainment.

Music was also an important part of Airdrie's social life. The Martinusen family was known throughout the district for their musical talents, playing at local socials and dances.

Community picnics and suppers were another chance to visit with friends and family. Suppers were held in the Airdrie United Church basement until the community hall was built. Weddings, amateur talent nights and Christmas concerts brought everyone together.

When a new family moved into town, neighbours stopped by and said hello with a plate of home-made cookies. Women always had to have a plate of sweets ready in case someone dropped over for tea.

A GROUP OF DANISH CANADIANS ENJOYING A PICNIC

## Box Socials

Box socials were a regular fundraiser that helped raise money for school, town or church projects.

Women donated boxes, each filled with a lunch they had prepared. Gentlemen bid on the boxes in hopes it was made by an eligible young lady with whom they could share the lunch. In fact, the boxes were often made by school girls, much to the surprise of the buyer. In any case, it provided a time for fun and friendship.

DANCE AT CROSSFIELD

## THE DIRTY THIRTIES

*Life in a dust bowl*

Airdrie did not escape the despair of the dirty thirties. People had to once again draw upon that inherent pioneer spirit, their resilience, and determination to continue with daily life.

When the stock market crashed in 1929, prices for farm products such as wheat and dairy fell dramatically. At the same time, drought swept over many agricultural regions of North America. Many people were left unemployed, homeless and feeling hopeless.

Records show that the Village of Airdrie provided relief (aid) in the form of lodging and meals for people down on their luck.[50] Those people with large gardens were fortunate to have enough to eat because they grew their own vegetables. Cabbage, carrots, peas, potatoes and turnips were staples.

People had faith in the land—confident that southern Alberta's rich soil would provide for them. However, with each successive year, the land became over-plowed and over-planted. Added to that, drought, grasshopper infestations and high winds caused the soil, which was exhausted of nutrients and moisture, to just blow away.

It was a hard lesson to learn, but the depression taught people about care of the land. New farming methods including "crop rotation" helped balance crop production with soil conservation. Farmers learned to diversify their crops and livestock.

The depression was a difficult time for everyone, but people picked themselves up, dusted themselves off and carried on, just as they always had done.

The depression ended in 1939, just as World War II began.

Glenbow Archives NC-6-12955b

## The Great Depression in Airdrie

*It was just pretty hard going. We were all in the same boat. Nobody had much in those days.*

*I recall people riding the rails. R.J. Hawkey would put them up in the (United) Church basement and feed them in the morning.*

*Dad raised a lot of garden stuff and traded it for groceries. Mother made butter and sold eggs.*

*During the depression, it cost more to take your hogs in to market than the money you'd get for them. I remember one farmer let his hogs loose.*

Chester Fowler
2007

### Grasshoppers

*It was in the dry years of the thirties that I wandered about on the wide open prairie. The brown grass, crisp and dusty, harboured a ravaging insect, the grasshopper... There were millions crawling everywhere.*

*How I wish someone had told me that there were people in this world that considered dried insects a delicacy. I would have dried those grasshoppers and sent them some just to cut down on the enormous numbers that invaded our prairie.*

*We learned to live and survive those dry years but are still haunted by the devastation of those ravaging insects.*

Jessie Bussey

# On the telephone line

## Airdrie gets wired!

With neighbours few and far between, rural folk enjoyed the contact that "barbed wire fence telephones" offered. This ingenious system worked by connecting telephone lines to a farmer's existing barbed-wire fence. The system was very localized with a limited range. A rain shower or a cow rubbing on the wire could affect reception!

The Alberta Government Telephone (AGT) system arrived in Airdrie in 1906. Airdrie's Les Farr was contracted to haul wire, poles and equipment. With hired men, wagons and teams, the lines were completed the following year, and Airdrie was "connected".[51]

Les Farr also had the contract to run the telephone exchange, which he did for 25 years. The telephone exchange building would later become Dusan's Clothing Store. In 1929, there were just 12 private phones in use, but by the 1960s, Airdrie had more than 100 private phones.[52]

The 1930s were challenging times for individuals and businesses, including the telephone company. AGT experienced financial difficulty and maintenance issues in the rural communities. Faced with the possibility of losing their government-run telephone service, villagers united in 1935 to form the Airdrie Mutual Telephone Company.[53] Local people purchased shares and became subscribers of the service in exchange for a phone and line connection to their property. Together, volunteers and hired repair men held work bees to repair damaged lines. The company served the Airdrie area until the early 1960s.[54]

A key local figure in the telephone story is certainly Mrs. Inez Clayton. Between 1932 and 1962, she served as Airdrie's telephone switchboard operator. The telephone office was located in the back of her house. She also served as the Assistant Secretary for the Airdrie Mutual Telephone Company for many years.

That's how the news traveled!

The rural telephone system was based on a "party line." Upwards of a dozen households would share one line. Everyone had their own ring, such as "one long and two shorts." Emergencies were signaled with one long ring. Party lines didn't offer much privacy. If somebody needed the line and it was busy, he'd just pick up the phone and say, "Please get off the line!" Some people enjoyed "rubber necking"—the art of listening in on other people's conversations. That's how the news traveled!

*My dad and my uncle used to talk to each other at 7 a.m. Officially, the telephone office didn't open until 8 a.m., so when Inez quit for the evening, she would leave their lines connected and in the morning they'd just pick up and start talking!*

Dan McKinnon
2008

HELEN MOORE STEWART AT TELEPHONE EXCHANGE, 1937

ETHEL WEIR AT THE AIRDRIE TELEPHONE OFFICE, 1958

# Purebreds and prizewinners

### Airdrie produces good stock!

Many local farmers and ranchers maintain a proud tradition of producing prize-winning crops and animals. From the early years of the 1900s, they entered their produce and livestock in agricultural shows. In addition to entering at local events, people participated in shows in British Columbia, Saskatchewan and beyond.

Known for exhibiting at the Calgary Stampede "forever," Chester Fowler and his family have raised prize-winning sheep in the Airdrie area since 1930. His purebred Suffolk sheep have been shown and sold throughout North America.[55]

The Hole family sold purebred Hereford bulls at the Calgary Bull Sale every year between 1934 and 1984, often fetching record prices.[56]

Hansons Ranches are also longtime Calgary Bull Sale participants, with 60 years of sales under their belt buckles.[57] The Hanson family was also winner of the 2005 BMO Financial Group and Calgary Stampede Farm Family of the Year Award.[58] Their cattle have been exported to countries around the world.

Incorporated in 1989, Bussey Seed Farms Ltd. grew out of Jim Bussey's first pedigreed crop, planted in 1943. A variety of barley, wheat and flax seeds have gone on to win awards for the Bussey's in Canada and the United States.[59]

Known for raising horses, the Tebb family farm was located on the outskirts of northeast Airdrie.[60] Cliff Tebb had the honour of leading the July 1 parade for many years, riding one of his beautiful palomino horses.

In 1922, the Webster family began raising prize-winning swine. Shown across Canada, some of the Webster-raised swine were included in a shipment of animals to China in the 1940s. D.M. Webster and G.A. Webster both served as directors of the Alberta Swine Breeders Association.[61]

CLIFF TEBB RIDING IN THE ANNUAL AIRDRIE PARADE

JIM AND JESSIE BUSSEY

CHESTER FOWLER (CENTRE) WITH HIS PRIZE-WINNING SHEEP

JIM HOLE

Postkarte

EXAMINED BY CENSOR DB/7

Mr. & Mrs. J. H. Lorimer

Gebührenfrei

Absender:
Vor- und Zuname:
LT. R. H. WALLACE
Gefangenennummer: 4039
Lager-Bezeichnung:
Kriegsgef.-Offizierlager VII B
BN. 1. COY. 3.
Deutschland (Allemagne)

Empfangsort: Airdrie
Straße: Alberta
Land: Canada.

Kriegsgefangenenlager

All Best
Wishes for
Christmas
1942. Richie

# WORLD WAR II

*Keeping the home fires burning, again*

With a sense of adventure in their hearts, Airdrie and area residents signed up for duty in the armed services. Dozens of local men (and a few women) headed overseas to unfamiliar lands to fight against a little-known enemy.

Airdrie residents were encouraged to do what they could for the war effort. The ladies of the local Red Cross Society would meet once a week to do piece quilting. With knitting needles in hand, school children made socks and caps for soldiers.

As a result of supplying produce and machinery to the war effort, farming and industry began to recover from the effects of the depression. As more men headed overseas, fewer were available to work the land. Farmers began to buy threshing machines and other equipment to take the place of diminished hired help. Machines helped increase production at a time when every bit of food made a difference.

On the home front, rations became the order of the day. The government sent out ration coupons for staples such as flour, sugar, coffee, butter and even gasoline. If you didn't have a coupon, you simply had to go without. Women relied on their ingenuity in the kitchen to cook and bake dishes without basic ingredients.

Families eagerly awaited the return of their young heroes. While many did return home safely, Airdrie lost several local boys. These included Albert Clayton, William Hegy, Frederick Larsen, John McNeill, Angus Ramsay, Armand Sabourin and Reuben Seefried.[62]

At the end of the war, some soldiers returned to their home towns with a new wife. Local soldiers and their war brides included Allan and Kitty Clayton, Clarence and Wilma Larsen, and Ian and Vivienne Weir.

ORMA AND ALBERT
CLAYTON, 1942

*I worked in the post office at that time. You knew when that letter came, you knew when you saw it, that he was called up (for service).*

Margaret (Carlson) Fowler
2007

TELEGRAM

pay

ED.

X 827 W 1 ST 1944.

No.

ended in. Office of Origin and Service Instruction

6.45 LONDON

PRIORI

FR        ISTRY

RE        ORM YOU THAT YOUR SON

= IS REPORTED TO H        IS

LIFE AS THE RESULT OF AIR OPERATIONS ON

DECEMBER 1944 (.) THE AIR COUNCIL EXPRE

PRO

THE DEFENCE MEDAL

1939 1945

WILLIAM HEGY DIED WHILE ON ACTIVE SERVICE, 1944

## Signing up for service

*A lot of the boys that had no jobs and nothing to eat traveled on the trains from one place to another, thought the service was great. They just joined up right away; they got good clothes and good food. A lot of them figured it would only be for two or three months or so, and they'd see the world and then go back home. It didn't turn out that way.*

Chester Fowler
2007

During World War II, air service personnel trained at the Airdrie Airport. These officers became a familiar sight around Airdrie and area.

*I was walking home from school one day—I was in grade one. This field ambulance with several servicemen in it stopped beside me and asked if I wanted a ride. Of course I said yes, I would take a ride from anybody. I told them to drop me off at the end of the driveway but they insisted on dropping me off at the house. My mother saw the ambulance and she comes screaming out of the house, thinking I was hurt. I had a great big grin on my face— proud and happy—I didn't like to walk!*

*I can also remember two planes crashed on our land. In one, the pilot was killed and the plane totally demolished. The other plane crash, they ran out of gas and flipped it over but they walked away from it.*

Dan McKinnon
2008

*During the war, the English Air Force soldiers (at the Airdrie Airport) would come into town. They were all upset that many of us were married!*

Opal Edwards, Hazel Clayton,
Margie Reid
2008

IAN AND VIVIENNE WEIR,
ENGLAND, 1945

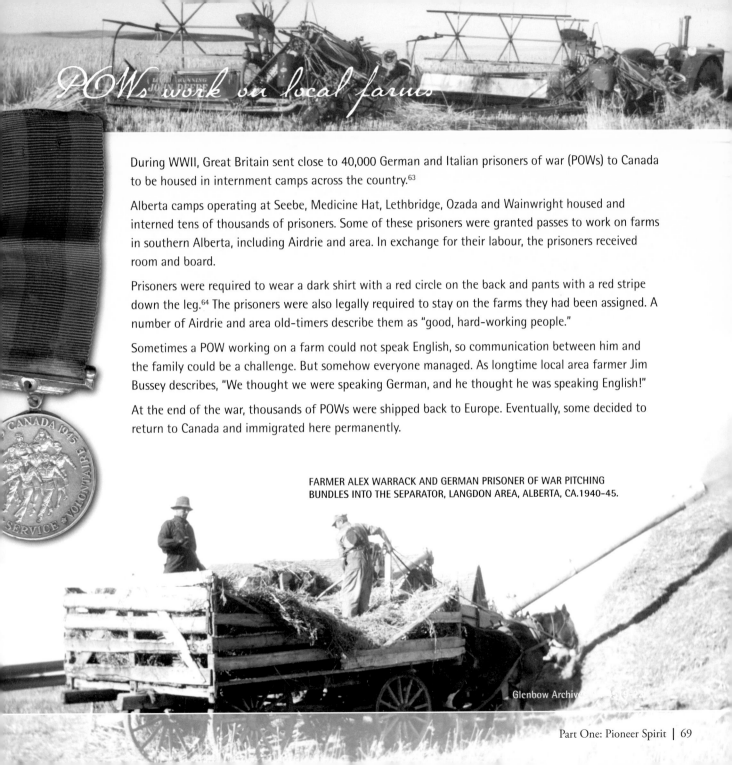

# POWs work on local farms

During WWII, Great Britain sent close to 40,000 German and Italian prisoners of war (POWs) to Canada to be housed in internment camps across the country.[63]

Alberta camps operating at Seebe, Medicine Hat, Lethbridge, Ozada and Wainwright housed and interned tens of thousands of prisoners. Some of these prisoners were granted passes to work on farms in southern Alberta, including Airdrie and area. In exchange for their labour, the prisoners received room and board.

Prisoners were required to wear a dark shirt with a red circle on the back and pants with a red stripe down the leg.[64] The prisoners were also legally required to stay on the farms they had been assigned. A number of Airdrie and area old-timers describe them as "good, hard-working people."

Sometimes a POW working on a farm could not speak English, so communication between him and the family could be a challenge. But somehow everyone managed. As longtime local area farmer Jim Bussey describes, "We thought we were speaking German, and he thought he was speaking English!"

At the end of the war, thousands of POWs were shipped back to Europe. Eventually, some decided to return to Canada and immigrated here permanently.

FARMER ALEX WARRACK AND GERMAN PRISONER OF WAR PITCHING
BUNDLES INTO THE SEPARATOR, LANGDON AREA, ALBERTA, CA.1940-45.

Glenbow Archive

## THE 1950s

*A time of prosperity*

The 1950s marked a time of renewed prosperity and growth. As local farms increased their level of mechanization, crop production increased. Farms benefited from connecting to the electrical grid. Electricity also meant the arrival of the latest fad to sweep the nation—television! Longtime Airdrie resident Lilly Jensen recalled being one of the first in Airdrie to have a TV set. Sometimes "everyone" would come over to watch![65]

Local businesses were thriving and new businesses arrived to take advantage of the booming economy. Owned by S.D. Southern and family, ATCO set up operations in old hangars at the Airdrie Airport in the mid-1950s. This occurred just after its Edmonton housing manufacturing facility was destroyed by fire, in the midst of its largest order to date. With the new operations at Airdrie, ATCO was able to fill its order on time.[66] ATCO would eventually become a big part of the Airdrie community, with hundreds of employees and numerous projects credited to its name.

THE JENSENS AND THEIR NEW TV!

In the 1950s, L.W. Shaw and Sons Construction Company was busy helping construct Airdrie businesses. Shaw-built projects included several garages and gas stations, the Roy Edwards Barber Shop and Pool Hall, and district schools.[67] At the same time, the Switzer family honey business gained recognition well beyond Airdrie and area.[68]

The business and infrastructure projects of the 1950s would help lay the foundation for the growth and development of Airdrie in the coming decades.

Glenbow Archives NA-5600-7208b

Agricultural field days at Victor Watson's farm (west of Airdrie) began in 1940. They were a major event for the community, with hundreds of people attending from near and far. Sponsored by the University of Alberta and the Lacombe Experimental Station, farmers and ranchers learned about the latest in crop varieties and animal husbandry. Taken in 1955, these photos show visitors viewing Hereford cattle and learning about experimental grain plots.[69]

Glenbow Archives NA-5600-6838a

By 1959, the pioneer spirit that had propelled Airdrie through its first half-century was as strong as ever, but beginning to take on a decidedly modern edge. Recognizing potential growth, entrepreneurs began to consider Airdrie a suitable place to locate their businesses. The provincial and municipal government built roads, schools and community facilities. Private developers constructed new housing developments that attracted additional people, particularly young families, to the community. The village population was about to explode.

This section looks at the pioneer spirit that has seen Airdrie emerge as the vibrant city it is today. Stories explore the people, businesses and events that have helped define Airdrie's second half-century.

*modern pioneer spirit*

*1959-2009*

## The village goes boom!

1959 proved to be the beginning of major expansion for Airdrie with the construction of the Built-Rite housing subdivision. Situated between 1st Avenue South, from Smith to Allen Street, it initiated an ambitious start to housing construction.[70] These affordable homes attracted more people to Airdrie. In just three short years, the subdivision helped double the village's population. In 1959, Airdrie had slightly more than 300 residents. By 1962, the population had doubled to approximately 600.[71]

In 1959, a water and sewage system was built. Storing water for emergencies, the water tower debuted on the landscape.[72] Silhouetted against the skyline, it immediately became Airdrie's landmark.

THE AIRDRIE WATER TOWER UNDER CONSTRUCTION

# Airdrie gets a fire brigade
## Sound the alarm!

In 1960, a volunteer fire-brigade was re-established in Airdrie. Local women were on standby to receive emergency calls and sound the siren.

An article in the *Rocky View News and Market Examiner* discusses the state of Airdrie's fire protection in the late 1950s:

*As and when the sewer and water installation is completed, the village will be in the position of having fire hydrants and no fire apparatus. It is proposed by your Council that some fire equipment will have to be purchased this year. This will also require a fire hall or the use of a suitable building.*

*The Municipality of Rockyview have offered the village an assortment of fire fighting equipment and the Council hope to receive it in the very near future.*

*At the present time, we have an agreement with the village of Crossfield for protection at a sum of $100.00 per year. This is very co-operative, but it does not give us the protection we require and it is my belief that the time is long overdue for our own fire department.*

*Rocky View News and Market Examiner*
*February 17, 1959*

## THE 1960s
*Paving the way for the future*

Prior to the 1960s, Airdrie's "downtown" would have been labeled rustic by today's standards. Only one block long, Main Street ended in a pasture that led to the village garbage dump (above photo). Streets were gravel and sidewalks were wooden boardwalks. Nose Creek often flooded in the spring, creating temporary ponds (and mud) for villagers to "enjoy."

By the 1960s, town improvement projects were underway and Airdrie's appearance began to change. Work on the creek channel helped reduce the chance of flooding. Sidewalks were poured at the same time as roads were paved. In 1963, George McDougall High School opened.[73]

In 1965, Airdrie resident and entrepreneur Frank Young developed his portable propane heating torch—the Tiger Torch. More than 40 years later, the company continues to operate from Airdrie. Now a division of Springbank Holdings Ltd., Tiger Torch shipments extend throughout North America.[74]

The year 1966 was a busy time in Airdrie. Council purchased land to extend Main Street a further two blocks north. The village built a civic centre to house council chambers, offices, an R.C.M.P. station and a garage for fire trucks and vehicle maintenance.[75] Airdrie residents received private garbage collection.[76] Prior to that, people burned their garbage in barrels in their backyards. Eventually the barrel would be full of ashes and refuse that didn't burn. Once the burn barrel was full, homeowners had to haul it down Main Street and empty it at the dump (near today's Main Street fire station).

GORDON MORRIS

PAT BENNETT

NORMAN MᶜCRACKEN

BOB EDWARDS

HUGH HAMILTON

WALTER MOEN

In 1965, Pat Bennett became the first
woman elected to village council.

ATCO FACTORY AT THE AIRDRIE AIRPORT, CA. 1960s

Glenbow Archives NA-5713-15

# Airdrie celebrates Canada's centennial
## Everyone loves a parade!

On July 1, 1967, Canada celebrated its centennial. To commemorate this special event, the Airdrie Lions Club planned a day of games, kids' races, a dance and a parade! Everyone in town worked to make it a memorable day. The parade included kids on bikes, colourful floats, cowboys and cowgirls riding horseback. The day was such a success that it became an annual event. Eventually, it grew to become the July 1 Parade and the five-day Airdrie Pro Rodeo.

Canada's centennial events provided a wonderful time for Airdrie to reflect on its pioneer spirit and celebrate all that the village had achieved in its short history.

## THE 1970s
### *The great leap forward*

During the 1970s, Airdrie made many great leaps forward. The first leap was east over the highway. In 1973, the Province of Alberta announced the purchase of land east of Highway 2 to develop a Highways and Transport Maintenance Branch along with a veterinary laboratory and agricultural specialists office.[77] This was followed in 1974, by the annexation of land east of the highway by the Town of Airdrie. With these "east lands," the time was right for town expansion. By the late 1970s, ATCO developed a community called Airdrie Meadows, and the Alberta Government developed Big Springs Estates. These communities were not without controversy as infrastructure needs could hardly keep pace with development. Many people also felt that the west side should be for residential development while the east side should be for business and light industry.

Many longtime Airdrie residents agree that the building of the six-lane Highway 2 (now QEII Highway) was a defining moment in the city's history. The original four-lane undivided highway through Airdrie became Edmonton Trail. The new highway, located just east of Edmonton Trail, allowed drivers to maintain full highway speeds while going through town. Road works in the 1970s saw the completion of the Highway 567 overpass and Yankee Valley Road/Big Springs Road underpass.[78] All of this road development made it even more convenient to live in Airdrie and work in Calgary or vice versa.

By 1974, Airdrie's population had topped 1000. Reaching this milestone made the village eligible to pursue town status with the provincial government. On May 1, 1974, the Village of Airdrie became the Town of Airdrie.[79] This achievement was 65 years in the making, as population growth had been slow until the 1960s.

The town's growth stretched the existing water system, which could not keep up with demand. A water line from Bowness on the Bow River to Airdrie was proposed. While the line was completed in 1976, Airdrie officially went on Calgary city water in 1977.[80]

Darrell Bennett was reeve at the time Airdrie became a town.

Opened in 1977, the new Town and Country Centre featured a curling rink, halls, public library, "Over 50 Club" room and kitchen. This complex replaced the old Quonset-style community hall building that had served Airdrie since 1948.

AIRDRIE'S MAIN STREET, 1974

# Industry comes to Airdrie

With housing and infrastructure projects in the works, entrepreneurs increasingly began to view Airdrie as a good place to establish a business.

In 1972, The DeFehr family of Winnipeg opened a furniture manufacturing plant in Airdrie.[81] In the years to come, this plant would provide employment for hundreds of people. Later the company became Palliser Furniture Ltd.

One business that seemed like a good idea at the time, but eventually caused a bit of a stink, was the Money's Mushrooms plant.[82] Built in the mid-1970s, the plant was located in a relatively isolated spot on Airdrie's east side. However, residential development soon encroached on the plant site. While the compost generated by the mushroom growing process was good for gardens, the resulting smell was not good for Airdrie residents! The plant moved to a site near Crossfield and Rol-Land Farms acquired it in 2005.[83] The company employs many people in the area.

By the mid-1970s, BURNCO Industries Ltd. expanded its concrete and rock operations to Airdrie. [84]

In the late 1970s, Propak Systems Ltd opened its Airdrie facility. Providing engineering, fabrication and construction services to the oil and gas industry, Propak continues to be an important employer in Airdrie.[85]

PALLISER FURNITURE

Money's
MUSHROOMS
MUSHROOMS
ON SPECIAL
TODAY
$3.50 PER
BASKET

PROPAK SYSTEMS LTD, AIRDRIE, JULY 2003

AIRDRIE'S EAST SIDE, 1978

## THE 1980s
*Finding an urban identity*

In the 1980s, new business and industry continued to find Airdrie a great place to locate their enterprises. Condillo Foods (a subsidiary of Old Dutch Foods Ltd.) opened at the start of the new decade, with a "first production run of tortilla chips!"[86] The company has since grown from just 15 employees to more than 100.[87]

With a growing population, Airdrie moved from a completely volunteer-run fire and emergency services crew to a mix of volunteers and paid staff. In the years to come, hired staff replaced volunteers and today, Airdrie Emergency Services employs several dozen people, with more soon to be on the payroll.

In 1984, the arts in Airdrie received a significant boost with the building of the Bert Church *Live* Theatre. Since then, the theatre has hosted a range of performers that have included local choirs, dance troops, Airdrie Little Theatre and the Calgary Philharmonic Orchestra.

On January 1, 1985, Airdrie became Alberta's 14th city.[88] Since becoming a town in 1974, Airdrie had grown to more than 10,000 residents. With such an increase of residents in such a short time, pressures on the infrastructure were bound to be an issue. However, new arrivals contributed by becoming active members of the community—joining clubs, volunteering with local organizations and connecting with neighbours. Airdrie residents were creating a new urban identity by building on a deeply rooted sense of community.

With a city full of young families, community building also considered the needs of local seniors. Opened in 1987, Airdrie's Bethany Care Centre gave longtime area residents the opportunity to stay in the city they had called home for so many years.[89]

Ron Davidson was mayor at the time Airdrie became a city.

CONDILLO FOODS

AIRDRIE EMERGENCY SERVICES

BETHANY CARE CENTRE

## Towerlane Mall

In the late 1970s, ATCO unveiled its plans for an enclosed shopping mall along Main Street, called the Towerlane Mall. Completed in 1982, some Airdrie residents recall thinking that "Airdrie had really made it" as a town now that it had a mall! Through the years, the mall has hosted many local clubs and causes. The 1st Airdrie Scouts have held their annual Kub Kar Rally here for many years. During the Christmas season, the Lioness Club used the mall as a donation depot for their Christmas hampers. Photos with Santa also helped everyone get in the Christmas spirit. Many seniors from the community enjoyed a daily walk in the mall, finishing their exercise with a chat and coffee with fellow mall-walkers. In 2008, Towerlane Mall received a facelift in keeping with an overall redevelopment strategy for downtown Airdrie.[90]

AERIAL VIEW OF AIRDRIE (TAKEN FROM THE NORTH LOOKING SOUTH), CA. 1980

Our most important resource

All firms, large or small, need one common resource—people. The youthful, energetic population of Airdrie provides business, industry, and commerce with an enviable cross-section from which to recruit. It is an interesting fact that 80 percent of our population is under the age of 35, which compares to the provincial average of 64 percent.

Town of Airdrie and District Chamber of Commerce publication, ca. 1981.

THE LAST STEAM TRAIN THROUGH AIRDRIE, 1955

Airdrie was built on the railway line. The first trains had steam locomotives, which took advantage of Airdrie's non-alkali creek water. Replaced by diesel locomotives, the last steam train rolled through Airdrie in 1955.[91] By the late 1960s, the self-contained passenger Dayliner was making the trip between Calgary and Edmonton. While a convenient way to travel, people expressed concerns. Many observed that the Dayliner's high traveling speed created real danger for motorists, especially at level crossings. Accidents were not uncommon and a number of deaths occurred.[92]

With better roads and increased car travel, use of the Dayliner began to wane. On September 5, 1985, the Dayliner had its last run.[93] With renewed talk of a high-speed rail link between Calgary and Edmonton in the 21st century, it would seem that the Dayliner may have been slightly ahead of its time!

THE LAST STEAM TRAIN THROUGH AIRDRIE, 1955

*At one time you had three choices of time to go to Calgary by rail and it was only fifty cents for a ride.*

Heloise Lorimer
1998

## Take the last train to Airdrie and I'll jump off at the station?!

Lifelong local Dan McKinnon is pretty sure he's the last person to have taken the passenger train to Airdrie. In the early 1960s, Dan found himself stranded in Calgary after a scheduled ride home didn't show up. Unconcerned, he made his way to the bus station, but found he'd missed the last bus of the day to Airdrie. He then headed to the train station only to have the ticket agent declare the train no longer stopped in Airdrie. But it did stop in Crossfield. It took some convincing, but Dan purchased a ticket and found a seat to enjoy the ride. Then, as the train slowed down while rolling through Airdrie, he made a jump for it!

# Snowstorm paralyzes city
## Say it isn't snow!

Every few years, southern Albertans experience a whopper of a spring storm. In mid-May 1986, Calgary, Airdrie and area enjoyed a blizzard that challenged everyone's sense of adventure. Record snowfall temporarily immobilized the area, leaving some people without power for two days and many roads impassable.

The blizzard hit the area with full force, but Airdrie weathered the storm with its usual tenacity. Hundreds of people became stranded along Highway 2. The Town and Country Centre provided refuge for 300 people.[94] A local state of emergency was declared as people worked to clear the roads and restore power. Residents of Airdrie provided stranded drivers with meals, shelter and respite from the storm. Airdrie's reputed spirit and generosity that prevailed during the crisis just confirmed what local residents already knew—Airdrie was Alberta's friendliest city!

If living without heat and power wasn't excitement enough, one Airdrie woman found herself in labour during the storm. She gave birth to a healthy baby girl at home while the blizzard raged outside.[95]

RALPH AND MARILYN MᶜCALL'S BACK YARD DURING THE STORM AND THEN JUST ONE WEEK LATER.

# Nose Creek Valley Museum

## Reflecting on the past

With more than 70 years of settlement history and community building to its name, the 1980s seemed the opportune time for Airdrie to reflect on its heritage and build a museum. The development of the Nose Creek Valley Museum was truly a joint venture, with residents of Airdrie, Balzac, Crossfield and surrounding communities offering their support. Funding from all levels of government plus financial donations from a variety of businesses made the building a reality. A sod-turning ceremony took place October 15, 1986, and the museum officially opened on June 11, 1988. Special guest, 89-year-old Mary Bushfield had the honour of cutting the ribbon.[96]

The museum tells the story of the Nose Creek Valley—from First Nations people to the coming of the railway and the founding of valley villages. The museum also includes an area for temporary exhibits, including shows by local artists.

# XV *Olympic Winter Games*
## The Airdrie connection

In 1988, Calgary hosted the XV Olympic Winter Games. This event created great excitement for all Albertans as "Olympic fever" swept the province. The 88-day Olympic Torch Relay offered Canadians a chance to "share the flame" by coming together to celebrate this great moment in sporting history.

Progressing toward Calgary, the Olympic Torch Relay made a memorable stop while passing through Airdrie. An impressive 15,000–20,000 residents come out to cheer the arrival of the Olympic torch.[97]

The city's connection to the torch continued during the opening ceremonies. A former Airdrie resident, Olympic speed skater Cathy Priestner Allinger, together with skier Ken Read, ran the torch into McMahon Stadium.

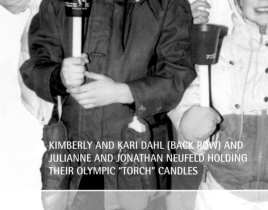

KIMBERLY AND KARI DAHL (BACK ROW) AND JULIANNE AND JONATHAN NEUFELD HOLDING THEIR OLYMPIC "TORCH" CANDLES

RALPH McCALL HANGING CALGARY '88 BANNER

CHARLOTTE BAUMANN PROUDLY CARRIES THE OLYMPIC TORCH INTO AIRDRIE

CLINT BILBEN WITH OLYMPIC MASCOTS HOWDY AND HEIDI

## THE 1990s
*Airdrie goes green*

Airdrie residents rang in the 1990s with an eye towards a "greener" future. Airdrie pioneered big and small programs that encouraged people to reduce, reuse and recycle. The annual Christmas tree burn gave way to the Christmas tree mulch program. The City introduced household garbage bag limits and developed a recycling program. Yellow fish painted near storm drains reminded people to keep harmful items out of the drains.

In 1990, a devastating fire rocked Palliser Furniture Ltd.[98] With a nearly inexhaustible supply of wood and chemicals acting as fuel, the fire burned and smoldered for days. The fire caused $7 million worth of damage and left 250 people out of work. Local firefighters worked tirelessly to extinguish the blaze, despite the dangerous inferno the fire had become. Palliser Furniture Ltd. chose to "rise from the ashes" and rebuild their Airdrie facility on the east side.

After countless volunteer hours, years of planning and support from Alberta's Urban Park Program, Nose Creek Park opened mid-September 1994.[99] The park soon became a focal point for community activities and recreation.

In late September 1994, traffic in Airdrie temporarily came to a halt as the Jensen barn was moved out of the city to make way for the community of Jensen Heights.[100] Built in 1931, the barn reflected Airdrie's pioneer past and rural roots within an urban landscape. After a slow but steady journey, the barn found a new home on the Jensen family farm west of Airdrie.

The decade ended with great excitement as the world headed toward the new millennium. The "Y2K computer bug" had a few people fearing it could be the "end of the world as we know it." At the stroke of midnight, Airdrie residents rang in 2000 with fireworks, dances and celebrations. Any worries of Y2K quickly vanished.

NOSE CREEK PARK

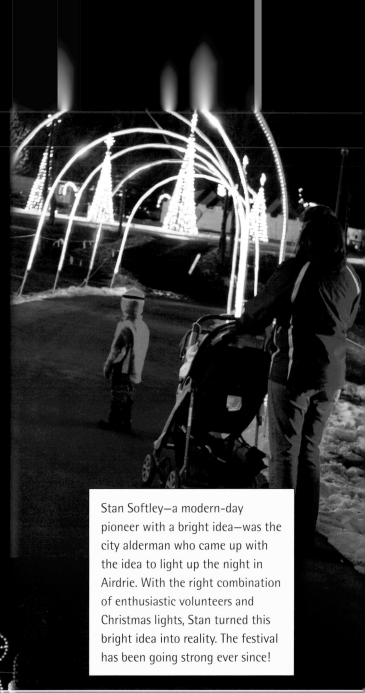

The Christmas season in Airdrie became much brighter with the inception of the annual Festival of Lights in 1996. Considered western Canada's largest outdoor "walk-through" light show, it truly dazzles. The success of the festival hinges on countless volunteer hours and community sponsorship.

Each year, the festival attracts thousands of visitors, who attend to enjoy the magic of the lights. Train rides, fireworks, music and hot chocolate around a bonfire add to the fun. Nose Creek Park serves as the picturesque setting.

Run by the Festival of Lights Society, the event relies on the work of community volunteer groups. In return for their time and enthusiasm, the volunteer groups receive an allocation from the proceeds to support their own activities.

An exciting change in 2007 was the introduction of light-emitting diode (LED) lights. This change meant that the festival uses far less energy, ensuring that the festival will shine brightly well into the future.[101]

Stan Softley—a modern-day pioneer with a bright idea—was the city alderman who came up with the idea to light up the night in Airdrie. With the right combination of enthusiastic volunteers and Christmas lights, Stan turned this bright idea into reality. The festival has been going strong ever since!

# Airdrie's global connection
## Linking people and cultures

In modern times, the pioneer spirit embodies adopting a global view extending well beyond the borders of this community. It entails exploring international relationships, appreciating different cultures and building businesses with an international scope. Since the 1980s, Airdrie has created "twinning" or sisterhood relationships with three cities around the world. Through these twinning programs, Airdrie has linked culturally, socially and economically to bridge vast distances and establish a global network.

# Twinning with Airdrie, Scotland

In June 1986, Mayor Ron Davidson visited Airdrie, Scotland. While visiting, he bought himself a kilt. Returning home, he subsequently wore it in the July 1 parade—with his cowboy hat. On the parade route, the combination didn't go unnoticed! The idea for twinning with Airdrie, Scotland, had been planted.

In November 1986, Grant McLean became mayor. Thinking it a natural combination, he further pursued the idea of a Scottish association. Airdrie issued an invitation to their Scottish namesake. Eight months later, in July of 1987, a receptive delegation arrived from Airdrie, Scotland, for official "twinning." The Lord Provost, Ed Cairns, his city administrator and four councillors made up the party. The Mayor and Provost signed the documents and the twinning was official. The Scottish group toured the city of Airdrie and the venues then being prepared for the 1988 Winter Olympics in Calgary.

In July 1988, Deputy Mayor Ralph McCall led an Alberta delegation of aldermen and their wives, city officials and business people on a return visit to Airdrie, Scotland. Tours of the Provost's chambers, the library, the ancient gaol (jail) and the museum were offset by tours of the snowball factory (candy maker) and one of the local distilleries.

Airdrie, Scotland, is an ancient commercial centre dealing in cotton and woolen weaving along with mining, coal, and iron. It is only a short distance from the deep-sea port of Glasgow. In the late 1990s, Airdrie, Scotland, was annexed and the official twinning with Airdrie, Alberta, came to an end. However, there remains an ongoing level of interest and friendship between the residents of the two namesake cities.[102]

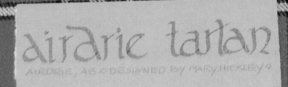

# Twinning with Yuto-Cho, Japan

The City of Airdrie and Yuto-Cho, Japan, began a sisterhood relationship on July 4, 1995. At the heart of the agreement was the sharing of two cultures through exchange and friendship. Airdrie and Yuto-Cho sought to develop economic, cultural and tourism opportunities, while at the same time, fostering respect between these two cities.

Each summer for 10 years, Airdrie families hosted Japanese students. Host families gave the students a taste of Airdrie life and friendships soon developed. In 2003, Airdrie students visited Yuto-Cho where they were embraced into the hearts and homes of the people of this warm community. In 2005, Yuto-Cho was annexed by nearby Hamamatsu and twinning activities lessened.[103]

YUTO-CHO STUDENTS SKATING (SOME FOR THE FIRST TIME!) AT THE TWIN ARENAS.

LARRY AND SHARON BILBEN WITH JAPANESE EXCHANGE STUDENT ICHIDO

# Twinning with Gwacheon City, South Korea

MAYOR DAN ONEIL IN SOUTH KOREA

OPENING AIRDRIE PARK IN GWACHEON CITY, SOUTH KOREA

In 1997, the City of Airdrie twinned with Gwacheon City, South Korea. This twinning program offers Airdrie and area residents the opportunity to share cultural experiences, develop friendships and explore economic opportunities. Each summer, Gwacheon students visit Airdrie. Many official visits have also occurred between the two cities. Such exchanges help foster understanding between cultures.

In 2002, Gwacheon City opened Airdrie Park—a beautifully landscaped green space that honours the twinning relationship. Airdrie reciprocated this gesture in July 2003, when Gwacheon Park opened within Nose Creek Park. Its location was selected because of the high visibility and prominence within the heart of Airdrie.

In Gwacheon Park, the stone anchoring the Korean arch and holding the plaque are made of sandstone. This stone symbolizes the foundation upon which Airdrie sits. It embodies the strength and endurance of the city's sisterhood. The central flowerbeds, the flagpoles and the sitting area incorporate the shape of a butterfly—a symbol for Gwacheon City. Roses have been planted to represent the provincial flower of Alberta, the Wild Rose, while the Mugunghwa is the national flower of Korea.

The year 2007 marked the 10th year anniversary of the city twinning. To celebrate this occasion, the City of Airdrie welcomed Mayor Yeo of Gwacheon, his wife, and honoured guests to Airdrie during the Canada Day long weekend. As a special gift to the City of Airdrie, Gwacheon City sent three pairs of handcrafted wood totem poles, each displaying a unique message to the community. The totem poles stand in Gwacheon Park and make an impressive addition to this city landmark.[104]

## THE 21st CENTURY
*Coming of age*

Unprecedented growth defined Airdrie's first decade of the 21st century as Alberta experienced yet another economic boom. Reminiscent of the westward wave of settlers one hundred years ago, thousands of people made their way to Alberta in search of better job opportunities. Airdrie's receptiveness to new businesses and new people, combined with its proximity to Calgary, made it an ideal community for relocating. Airdrie has become one of the fastest growing cities in Canada. In just seven years, Airdrie experienced 50% growth. The population of just over 20,000 in 2001, increased to more than 30,000 by 2008.[105]

Such rapid growth and expansion impacted locally established businesses—sometimes in unexpected ways. With Alberta's latest boom in full swing, production costs were rising. Competition for skilled labour created a demand that increased daily wages. Longtime local employer, Palliser Furniture Ltd announced it was closing its doors in 2007. The company redistributed its workload to branches in Winnipeg, Manitoba, and Mexico.[106]

Big-box stores opened on the north and south end of the city, anchoring the Main Street commercial corridor. In 2008, one of Airdrie's oldest buildings, the Old Hotel, closed its doors for the last time.

Also in 2008, local athletes proved they had the right mix of skill and determination to qualify for the Beijing 2008 Summer Olympic Games. Airdrie swimmer Joel Greenshields secured his spot on the men's Canadian national team.[107] Samantha Cools helped bring BMX racing to the Olympics for the first time.[108]

In the latter half of 2008, the world entered into a time of severe economic slowdown. For Albertans, this slowdown represents another turn in the cycle of boom and bust.

# Airdrie celebrates Alberta's centennial

On September 1, 2005, Airdrie residents enjoyed Alberta's centennial celebration honouring the founding of the province. The day was jam-packed with fun events for young and old. Activities included a turn-of-the-century fashion show, a strawberry tea, museum tours, music performances, a farmers' market and an evening fireworks display. Airdrie residents also contributed to a mini–time capsule that became part of a province-wide capsule, to be unsealed during Alberta's bicentennial year in 2105.

**2005**
Alberta Centennial

*One Hundred Years*
of Motoring in Alberta

**1911 CADILLAC**

# Hockeyville

## In Airdrie, nobody sits on the bench!

Nothing says Canada quite like early mornings, cold arenas, mounds of stinky equipment and kids playing hockey!

In 2006, the CBC, Kraft Canada, the NHL and the NHL Players Association sponsored "Hockeyville." Described as a Canada-wide search for the community that best embodies the spirit of hockey, Hockeyville was looking for towns with a lot of heart but limited funds to complete arena repairs and buy equipment.[109] The winning town would receive $50,000 in upgrades to the local arena, $10,000 worth of hockey equipment and host an NHL exhibition game.

A team of dedicated community volunteers calling themselves the Prairie Pond Posse organized Airdrie's application. On March 29, 2006, CBC aired the first episode of Kraft Hockeyville. The community held their collective breath waiting to hear whether the Airdrie application had made it through the first round. To everyone's great delight, Airdrie remained within the top 50, selected from more than 400 entries. With a game-winning theme, "Nobody sits on the bench," and a lot of local support, Airdrie's application was bound to get the judges' attention!

In the weeks to come, the competition intensified as communities across Canada faced-off against one another. Judging continued through a series of video presentations and call-in voting. The competition also included a "surprise project." Home Depot gave the top 25 finalists $2500 worth of products to spruce up their arenas. Working within a two-hour time limit, more than 200 local volunteers transformed Airdrie's Twin Arenas with new landscaping and murals. This was community spirit in action!

The final outcome of Kraft Hockeyville? Airdrie scored a top 5 finish and netted the community $10,000 worth of new hockey equipment. Salmon River, Nova Scotia, took home the top prize, but for many local residents, Airdrie truly is Hockeyville![110]

PRAIRIE POND POSSE (L TO R): ROB ING, AL JONES, MICHELLE CALLOWAY, PETER BROWN, MURRAY BUCHANAN IS SITTING IN PASSENGER SEAT

Part Two

*community pride*

AIRDRIE'S BASEBALL TEAM, 1957

*the people make the city*

Airdrie's people make the city a great place to live, work and play. Whether a sixth-generation resident or a new arrival, young or old, Airdrie's mix of residents have created a vibrant and friendly city of which they can be proud.

People have contributed to the community in countless ways. The city is known for its volunteerism. People donate their time to many causes, including those related to youth, seniors, sports, arts and culture, local events and city beautification. What unifies all volunteers is their commitment to make a difference in the community.

Many others shaped the city through the businesses they've run or the jobs they've done. Whether called colourful characters, prominent people or fine folks, all have worked to make a difference.

Some people settled in Airdrie their entire lives; others just passed through. Whatever the length of stay, their contributions, influence, and impact linger. Through stories and pictures, the people of Airdrie are celebrated.

## DR. W.F. EDWARDS 1879–1940

*Healing the sick*

In the early days of settlement on the prairies, country doctors were often few and far between. When a village did have a doctor, he had to be a jack of all trades—able to set broken bones, deliver babies and tend to scrapes and bruises.

Airdrie's country doctor was Dr. William Ferdinand Edwards, but he was better known as Fred.[1] After studying medicine at McGill University in Montreal, Dr. Edwards came west and opened his practice in Airdrie in 1907. With $200 start-up money from his father, Dr. Edwards purchased everything he needed to run his practice. This included all necessary medical instruments and a horse and buggy for making house calls.

In 1908, Dr. Edwards met and married Miss Anna McCracken, a teacher at the Dry Creek School west of Airdrie. Together they had four children, two of which survived into adulthood. Descendents of Fred and Anna Edwards still reside in the Airdrie area today.

As the only doctor between Calgary, Cochrane and Irricana, Dr. Edwards soon found himself very busy. In 1910, he moved into a bigger shop that could handle a larger supply of drugs. He also installed a soda fountain and sold a variety of goods, including glass and chinaware, pipes, toys, stationery, cold creams and talcum powders —definitely a one-stop shop!

Dr. Edwards' story is one of friendship and medical service to the community. In June 1940, he contracted a severe "strep" infection. He was taken to the Holy Cross Hospital in Calgary for treatment. He was not able to be saved. Dr. Edwards passed away at the age of 61 years.

DR. EDWARDS – BACK ROW, FAR RIGHT

Formula for 2 weeks

milk 5 ozs.
water 15 ozs.
cream 1 oz. — fairly rich cream 25 or 40%
sugar ½ oz.
at two weeks allow baby
feed 7 times in 24 hours.
lightly more than 2 ozs.

Formula for 1 m...

milk 7 ozs.
water 14 ozs.

DR. EDWARDS' FORMULA RECIPE FOR A TWO-WEEK-OLD BABY

ANNA EDWARDS AND DR. EDWARDS INSIDE THEIR STORE

# HELOISE LORIMER

*Witness to history*

Well into her 90s, it is safe to say that Heloise Lorimer has witnessed phenomenal changes in this city.[3] Making her debut in 1912 as Heloise Van Sickle, she has watched Airdrie grow from a village of 100 people to a city of 30,000.

In 1918, Heloise began attending Airdrie's one-room schoolhouse. Reading, writing and arithmetic were the order of the day. Heated by a stove in the middle of the room, the school would stay relatively warm in winter, but the water pump would often freeze up. As a schoolgirl, Heloise enjoyed playing baseball and hockey, even if it meant playing with the boys!

Heloise married Jim Lorimer in 1931 and they raised three boys. Jim operated a garage across the road from their house for 50 years, until his death in 1971. Their house was always a busy place with friends stopping by for coffee, cake and conversation.

Heloise has always been an active member of the community. Her love of baseball continued into adulthood and she played in competitive leagues. Heloise holds the distinction of being Airdrie's first school bus driver. The bus was actually an old Cadillac, but it seemed to do the job! In the 1960s, Airdrie's volunteer fire brigade depended on Heloise and Ruth Fletcher to answer the "fire phone." On standby day and night, the ladies were responsible for sounding the siren in case of fire. Heloise was also a member of Airdrie United Church, where she taught Sunday school and was part of the women's group.

On the occasion of Alberta's centennial in 2005, Heloise, along with a handful of Airdrie residents, received a Centennial Medal for contributions to community.

AIRDRIE'S FIRST SCHOOL BUS, 1945

AIRDRIE GIRLS BASEBALL TEAM 1930s
BACK ROW L TO R: UNKNOWN, OPAL (ONSTAD) EDWARDS, KEREN (McCRACKEN) LUCK,
HELOISE (VAN SICKLE) LORIMER, MABEL (POLE) ONEIL
FRONT ROW L TO R: MARGARET (McCRACKEN) KOLSTAD, BERNIE (EDWARDS) MORISON,
HAZEL (ONSTAD) CLAYTON, GLADYS (HEGY) FLETCHER

HELOISE LORIMER CELEBRATES HER 96th BIRTHDAY.

Originally homesteading near Yankee Valley in 1906, the Van Sickle family eventually moved into Airdrie and ran the Airdrie Supply Store (which they acquired from Dr. Edwards). The storefront sign said it all—"groceries, dry goods, boots, shoes, flour & feed."

## RALPH LEWIS McCALL  1925–1995

*Teacher, leader, friend*

Ralph McCall is remembered for his deep commitment to his family, his students and the community.[4]

Born in Morrin, Alberta, Mr. McCall spent his formative years in Rich Hill, Missouri. In 1943, his family returned to Alberta, at which time Mr. McCall attended the University of Alberta. In 1948, he received a Bachelor of Education and began teaching in Acme. He would eventually receive a Master of Education degree in 1956.

In 1958, he married Marilyn Gale (also a teacher) and together they raised three children—two girls and a boy. In 1964, they moved from Red Deer to Airdrie, where Mr. McCall would spend the next 21 years teaching at George McDougall and Bert Church high schools. In 1985, he retired from teaching.

Despite his busy schedule as a teacher, Mr. McCall also found time to delve into the world of local politics. In 1976, he was elected to council in a by-election. He then went on to serve as Deputy Mayor from 1977–1989 at which time, he retired.

Mr. McCall had a love of history that resulted in guest columns on local history in the *Airdrie Echo*. He shared his knowledge by giving tours at the Nose Creek Valley Museum to hundreds of students. He was known as an avid gardener and birdwatcher and enjoyed spending time with his grandchildren. Mr. McCall sang in church choirs for more than 40 years, including many years with the Airdrie United Church choir.

Ralph McCall has left a lasting legacy in Airdrie, which is recognized in the school bearing his name. A large mural in the school's entrance commemorates his achievements and the people and places he touched through the years.

THE OLYMPIC FLAME ARRIVES IN AIRDRIE, FEBRUARY 1988

RALPH McCALL WITH GRANDCHILDREN DAYNA AND SHANTAL

GRANT McLEAN, RALPH McCALL, AND REDVERS PERRY IN THE JULY 1st PARADE IN THE LATE 1980s

## BRIAN JACKSON

*Ground control to Mr. Jackson*

Teacher Brian Jackson's enthusiasm for all things space-related is well known at Ralph McCall School and throughout the community.[5] As a self-described "space geek," Mr. Jackson's passion for space travel has meant his students have enjoyed "close encounters of the astronaut-kind."

In 2005, a group of students from Ralph McCall School plus one student from Chestermere Lake Middle School were given the unique opportunity to speak with an astronaut aboard the International Space Station. Communicating via amateur ham radios, the students had a 10-minute timeline to ask their questions and absorb the thrill of the experience.

Selected from more than 1,000 applications, Mr. Jackson had his own thrilling space experience in 2007, by attending the U.S. Space and Rocket Centre in Huntsville, Alabama. The space camp program included classroom and laboratory time, in which participants learned about new strategies for teaching math and science.

Brian Jackson's commitment to education and his students is clear in everything he does. With his infectious enthusiasm, Mr. Jackson is no doubt helping to shape a future generation of scientists and astronauts.

# PAUL BRANDT

*Small towns and big dreams*

The name Paul Brandt has been synonymous with the Canadian country music scene for more than a decade.[6]

Paul was born on July 21, 1972, in Calgary, Alberta. He spent his younger years growing up in Airdrie, which was, as he describes, "still a very small town" at the time.

A win at the 1992 Calgary Stampede's Youth Talent Showdown was Paul's first big step on the path toward superstardom. Fast forward to 2009 and his résumé boasts countless awards, including the Canadian Country Music Association Male Artist of the Year.

In addition to his music, Paul Brandt is recognized for his commitment to charity work through his involvement with the Alberta Children's Hospital Foundation, World Vision and Samaritan's Purse. After living in Nashville for a number of years, Paul has returned to southern Alberta and calls the foothills west of Calgary home.

*...Doesn't matter where I go*
*This place will always be my home...*
**Excerpt from Paul Brandt's "Alberta Bound"**

PAUL BRANDT IN BELIZE FOR SAMARITAN'S PURSE OPERATION CHRISTMAS CHILD

# LINDA BRUCE

*Airdrie's centennial mayor*

Although born and bred Nova Scotian, it is safe to say that after more than 20 years living "out west," Mayor Linda Bruce can now be considered a real prairie dweller.[7]

On December 31, 1990, Linda Bruce rang in the New Year by moving from Lethbridge to Airdrie; and while her New Year's resolution was not "to become a politician," she ventured into the political arena soon thereafter. Initially becoming involved with the Airdrie Recycling Committee, Linda was elected to City Council in 1995 and served three terms as Alderman before being elected Mayor in 2004. She was acclaimed in 2007.

With a passion to make a difference, Linda was elected Chair of the Calgary Regional Partnership at its inception in 2004. She also chairs regional land-use planning, waste and water committees. This reflects her dedication to cooperation and problem-solving across municipalities.

Mayor Bruce is very excited about Airdrie's focus on growth and sustainability as one of three municipalities in Alberta to participate in The Natural Step Program. To Mayor Bruce, Airdrie's rapid growth has been a unique challenge that she is meeting head-on with passion and determination. Mayor Bruce describes Airdrie's growth as "very exciting— the new businesses and families coming to town are wonderful."

Mayor Bruce calls Airdrie a "little gem" and enjoys the direct contact with the community that her position offers. Linda says, "One of my favourite things to do as mayor is attending all the different events that go on in and around Airdrie. I am honored to be the Mayor of Airdrie and realize I am very fortunate."

# TIM HARRIMAN

*Cycling for a cause—The spokeman tour for childhood cancer*

For many people, cycling to the corner store is a major feat. Now imagine cycling across Canada—all 7619.4 kilometres of it! Tim Harriman did just that in an effort to raise funds and awareness for the Childhood Cancer Foundation of Canada.[8]

Growing up in Airdrie, Tim was heavily involved with sports, including hockey, soccer, baseball and swimming. After a hockey tryout in September 2002, Tim was clearly ill and taken to hospital. At just 14 years of age, he was diagnosed with a type of cancer called Acute Lymphoblastic Leukemia (ALL). His prognosis was poor and he was to endure nearly three years of difficult treatment.

Within two months of Tim's diagnosis, the people of Airdrie raised $20,000 to help the family through this difficult time. Tim recalls, "The first year of my sickness, the freezer was always full of meals people had prepared for us. The community was very supportive."

During his treatment at the Alberta Children's Hospital, Tim met other young cancer patients. It was at this time, he began to dream about cycling across Canada to raise funds for childhood cancer. With support from family, friends, the community and sponsors, the dream became a reality on June 3, 2007, when he left Victoria, British Columbia, and headed for Newfoundland. By the time he reached St. John's on August 24, 2007, Tim had met with countless childhood cancer patients and their families, ridden over some challenging terrain, survived wild weather and raised over $100,000.

Today, Tim continues to look for ways to make a difference in the community. While his cross-Canada bike tour may be over, Tim's journey has only just begun, as he looks to inspire and spread a message of hope to families affected by childhood cancer.

## ROBIN BURWASH

*Fan's favorite cowboy*

Robin Burwash got on his first bucking horse at the tender age of 13.[9] Attending George McDougall High School with fellow cowboy and friend Jim Dunn, the two joined the newly formed Alberta High School Rodeo Association. They started a local high school rodeo club. With support from the school's student union, they purchased a bucking barrel to practice their riding skills.

After attending Montana State University on a rodeo scholarship, Robin went on to win numerous bareback championships, including top-honours at the Calgary Stampede. In 1990, he was named the Fan's Favourite Cowboy at the National Finals Rodeo in Las Vegas, Nevada. Retiring from competition in 1994, Robin worked as the Rodeo/Ranch Manager of the Calgary Stampede between 2002 and 2006. While in this position, he helped organize the first $1 million rodeo.

## RON DAVID

*Keeping it all in the family*

Ron David's adventures in chuckwagon racing began in 1963 at the age of 18. Ron's father, Wilbur, and brothers Les, Roy, Butch and Larry, all had a connection to the world of chuckwagon racing.[10] It is safe to say that the Davids have done a great job of keeping the sport in the family!

In 1965, Ron David made his first trip to the Calgary Stampede.[11] In the following years, he enjoyed racing and winning at events throughout western Canada. In 1977, he was runner-up for the Calgary Stampede's esteemed Guy Weadick Award. In 2000, Ron made his final turn around the Stampede's "half-mile-of-hell." In 2001, the World Professional Chuckwagon Association honoured Ron with the inaugural George Normand Lifetime Builders Award.

In 2008, the David family legacy continues with Ron's two grandsons participating in chuckwagon racing, with Chad Fike riding as an outrider and Jordie Fike starting as a driver.[12]

## JIM DUNN

*From little britches to bucking broncs*

Born in 1955 and raised on a farm west of Balzac, Jim Dunn has lived in the Balzac/Airdrie area all his life. In the early 1970s, Jim entered the cow-riding event at his first rodeo—the Black Diamond Little Britches Rodeo.[13] By the 1980s, Jim had graduated to riding bigger and tougher stock—bareback horses. In 1980, 1985 and 1986, he won the Canadian Champion Bareback Rider title. He also qualified for the National Finals Rodeo six times.[14] With these and many other awards under his belt buckle, Jim was inducted into the Canadian Professional Rodeo Hall of Fame in 2002. Two years later, Jim received the Cowboy of the Year Award from the Canadian Professional Rodeo Association.[15]

## JIM NEVADA

*Driving all over the world*

Airdrie's own Jim Nevada began his cowboy career working as a barn boy for chuckwagon driver Ron David.[16] He then jumped on a horse and started as an outrider. In 1984, he added "chuckwagon driver" to his résumé.

Through the years, Jim's list of accomplishments has grown to include many awards and prizes. In 1999, Jim received the prestigious Guy Weadick Memorial Award, which is given annually to a competitor that embodies the spirit of the Calgary Stampede.

Conjuring up images of "spaghetti western" meeting Middle-Eastern falafel, Jim headed to the Sultanate of Oman in 2005. With five refurbished chuckwagons shipped from Alberta, he accepted an invitation issued by the Omani government to introduce this horse-enthusiastic country to a real wild-west sport! The following year, he co-presented a lecture on chuckwagon races at the Smithsonian Institute in Washington, D.C.

*familiar, favourite and*

*unforgettable places*

In every city, there are places that bring people together, promote a sense of neighbourliness or serve as a symbol of the community. In Airdrie, some of those places have come and gone, but their importance in the community remains. Other landmarks still stand today as special reminders of Airdrie's growth and development over the past 100 years.

## ATLAS LUMBER COMPANY

*Timber!*

Building a village from the ground up required hard work, perseverance and lumber—a lot of lumber! Villagers built homes, barns, corrals, fences, boardwalks, businesses and more.

Airdrie's lumberyard opened for business in 1901.[17] A.E. Bowers and Thomas Fletcher managed the yard for the first four years, when George Hatt took over until his death in 1911. That year, the Bowman-Sine Lumber Co. of Minneapolis, Minnesota, bought the Airdrie yard. It became known as the Atlas Lumber Co. The company owned a number of yards in southern Alberta, including those located in Calgary, Crossfield and Lethbridge.

Known for its generosity, the company donated to Airdrie's Sports Day. At Christmas, they gave turkeys to the married employees. If a farmer couldn't pay for lumber with cash, they often accepted grain as payment. Advertisements for the Atlas Lumber Co. appeared in the local newspaper, the *Airdrie Recorder*.

Eventually, the Atlas Lumber Co. name became Revelstoke (now Rona). In 1968, Revelstoke donated the Atlas Lumber Company shed and office to Heritage Park Historical Village in Calgary. It has since undergone renovations and helps the park visually tell the story of a typical small town lumberyard in western Canada.

Form No. 3401-3M-7-26

**M**

4

# ATLAS LUMBER COMPANY, Limited
### BUILDING MATERIAL

Yard _____ 192 _

Ent. Repor

ters, Calgary   Est. No. _____  Accou

| Grade | Kind | FEET | |
|-------|------|------|---|

**GEO. HATT**
Dealer in All Grades of
**Lumber**
And
BUILDING MATERIALS
XXX Shingles $3 per M.
**All Prices Right.**

*The Airdrie News*
*July 16, 1908*

Atlas Lumber Co. also sold coal.
Customers weighed their load on a
truck scale.

at Head Office   TOTAL $

TOTAL DUE

30 days from above date.

# OLD HOTEL

*If those walls could talk*

For more than 100 years, The Old Hotel on the corner of Centre Avenue and Main Street was a fixture on the Airdrie landscape.

In 1902 or 1903, Dan McDonald, believed to be the first owner, moved an existing building onto the site. The Airdrie Hotel was open for business.[18]

Through the years, the hotel changed hands many times and underwent extensive renovations. It was everything from bachelor's quarters for men doing construction work in early Airdrie to a 25-bed hospital during the 1918/1919 influenza epidemic.[19]

The hotel also served as a social hub for Calgarians looking for an excuse to enjoy an evening's outing. During prohibition, between 1916 and 1923, the "beverage room" closed but the hotel remained open.[20] Between 1928 and 1957, mixed-drinking (men and women having a drink together) was banned in Calgary, so people from the city would come to The Old Hotel to enjoy mixed-drinking.[21,22]

In February 2008, Airdrie bid farewell to The Old Hotel. Backhoes and bulldozers made quick work of demolishing the old building. A new building will stand on this same spot, which holds a special place in Airdrie's collective memory.

THE OLD HOTEL, CA. 1950s

# THE OLD HOTEL

Great Improvements are being made in the hotel. The bar-room is to be moved to the room formerly used as a sitting room and the former bar-room used as a sitting room. A fine new mirrored bar with all the latest fixtures has been put in and will soon be ready for use.

*The Airdrie News*
September 22, 1909

Airdrie Hotel
Home-like quarters, good service and wholesome meals

*The Airdrie Recorder*
Advertisement 1924

*The parlor was the 'piece de resistance' together with the 'best rooms,' which adjoined it. There was a piano, thick carpet and nice furniture in the parlor, also a plate rail around the top part of the walls which were loaded with handsome china.*[23]

Ada Ryan
1962

DEMOLISHING THE OLD HOTEL, FEBRUARY 2008

THE OLD HOTEL

TAVERN    HUB PUB    BILLIARDS

# GRAIN ELEVATORS

*True prairie giants*

Known by many names, including "wheat kings," "prairie giants," "prairie sentinels" and "prairie castles," grain elevators are truly a symbol of western Canada and farming life.

Built in 1904–1905, Airdrie's first grain elevators were relatively small, but very important.[24] They established Airdrie as a hub for grain shipment. Just a few years later in 1909, the Alberta-Pacific elevator was built and the National Grain elevator was completed in 1927.[25,26]

In 1929, the Alberta Wheal Pool built its first elevator in Airdrie.[27] In the decades to follow, the Pool built two additional elevators and bushel capacity increased accordingly.

As the 20th century marched on, the Airdrie elevators were used less and less, as area farmers sent their grain to Beiseker, Carstairs and Indus.

The last of Airdrie's grain elevators were torn down July 31, 2000, bringing an end to nearly 100 years of this prairie symbol.

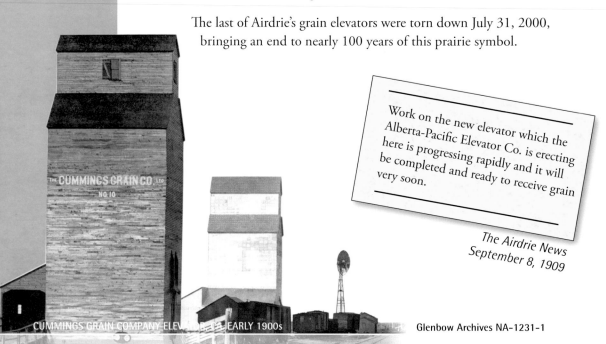

Work on the new elevator which the Alberta-Pacific Elevator Co. is erecting here is progressing rapidly and it will be completed and ready to receive grain very soon.

*The Airdrie News*
*September 8, 1909*

CUMMINGS GRAIN COMPANY ELEVATOR IN EARLY 1900s

Glenbow Archives NA-1231-1

In 1943, the Airdrie C.P.R. station burned down. At the time, we had no fire-fighting equipment. While the station burned to the ground, we were able to save the grain elevator. We formed a bucket brigade and hauled water from the reservoir to the fire. When the water hit the wall of the elevator, the steam was so thick, we could hardly see. At times, the sap in the wood boiled out and ran down the side of the elevator. After the fire died down and everyone was gone except those of us on the bucket brigade, we noticed the stationmaster sitting on the north side of the platform holding on to the bug (the telegraph sender button). He had on one shoe, his pants and shirt. I didn't know his name, but he looked very sad—he had lost everything he owned.

Glen Hutchings
2008

1.

2.

3.

AIRDRIE'S LAST GRAIN ELEVATORS – GOING... GOING... GONE

# AIRDRIE CEMETERY

*History in headstones*

Established in 1908, a walk through Airdrie Cemetery reveals a century of history and family heritage.

Etched onto headstones are the names of founding pioneers and longtime resident families. This includes Arthur E. and Esther Bowers—owners of Airdrie's first house and store— and Airdrie's first blacksmith, Tom Flett.

The headstones reveal many stories, including that of a young man named Jack Dawson. In 1912, he was found wandering the countryside nearly frozen to death. Mr. Dawson was treated by Dr. Edwards before being sent to Calgary for more treatment. Unfortunately, Mr. Dawson soon passed away and was buried in the Airdrie Cemetery. His grave is marked with a marble headstone that his mother and sister had sent over from Scotland.[28]

When the Spanish influenza epidemic hit Airdrie in 1918–1919, it claimed the lives of only four Airdrie residents. They are buried in the Airdrie Cemetery.

The Airdrie Cemetery truly offers a glimpse into the past and the people that shaped a city.

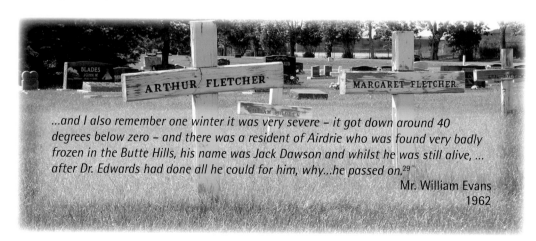

*...and I also remember one winter it was very severe – it got down around 40 degrees below zero – and there was a resident of Airdrie who was found very badly frozen in the Butte Hills, his name was Jack Dawson and whilst he was still alive, ... after Dr. Edwards had done all he could for him, why...he passed on.*[29]

Mr. William Evans
1962

# AIRDRIE UNITED CHURCH

*Hymnbooks and history*

Private homes, including those of A.E. Bowers and William Croxford, hosted Airdrie's first church services.[30] In 1903, services moved to the newly constructed Methodist Church. As Airdrie's population grew slowly but surely, the congregation outgrew the little church. In 1922, a new Methodist church was constructed. After the congregation moved to the new location, the old church became a school.

In 1925, the Methodists became the United Church of Canada. For many years, this was Airdrie's only church and a number of religious denominations held their services here. The church played an important role in Airdrie—not only as a spiritual hub, but also as a village gathering place. Weddings, funerals, suppers and concerts brought people together in celebration and community.

Church suppers were a particularly popular event. Originally held in the church basement, these suppers became so well attended, they moved into the community hall when it was built in 1948. During the 1950s and 1960s, the church hosted these suppers. With up to 500 attendees over the course of an evening, the feast was organized and served in the hall basement. Women prepared all food at home. Everything then had to be transported to the hall. That included the water for clean-up, as there was no running water in the hall. The dishwater got to be pretty thick before more heavy buckets of clean water were heated and ready for use![31]

As one of Airdrie's remaining "old time" public buildings, the church connects people to Airdrie's historic landscape.

AIRDRIE UNITED CHURCH, CA. 1930

## THE HANDY LUNCH
*Take-out with a twist!*

Ask any longtime resident of Airdrie for memories of old Main Street and most are sure to mention the Handy Lunch, better known as Jock's.[32] Owned by Louie Tong, the restaurant offered take-out and later dine-in food. Louie also sold penny candy, pop and cigarettes.

Getting take-out from Jock's was a different experience from that of today. When diners picked up their food, they took home their meal on china plates. People ate their meal, washed the plates and then returned them to Jock's—certainly a system based on trustworthiness!

As with a number of businesses on Main Street, the restaurant was on street level while the family lived upstairs. Louie lived by himself for many years waiting for his family to come over from China. One son arrived in the early 1950s; the other two sons and his wife came over in the early 1960s. Sadly, in the late 1960s, Louie and his wife were in a car crash on their way into Calgary. Louie was injured and his wife was killed.

**Handy Lunch**
*Louie Tong*

**Eat here after the dance**
**Palm Ice Cream, Candies, Tobacco**
**Always open for service**

Tested recipes from the
Ladies of Group 2
Airdrie United Church

**We always just called it Jock's!**

In 1923, an advertisement appeared in the *Airdrie Recorder* newspaper for the

**"Airdrie Café, Louis Tong proprietor".**

In 1924, another advertisement appeared for the

**"Airdrie Café and Rooming House, meals – at any hour, day or night".**

It is unclear as to when the restaurant name changed from the Airdrie Café to the Handy Lunch or how Louie Tong got the nickname Jock.

During the depression...

[In 1933] These were the 'hard years' and it was moved and seconded [by Village Council] that L. Tong should provide meals costing no more than 25¢ for those on relief. (In November, a bill as large as $140 was paid to Louie Tong for feeding relief people). [In 1934] Louie Tong was paid $35 for meals.[33]

AIRDRIE STREET VIEW, CA. 1907-1909     Glenbow Archives PA-3689-335

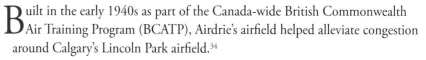

# AIRDRIE AIRPORT

*Ready for takeoff*

Built in the early 1940s as part of the Canada-wide British Commonwealth Air Training Program (BCATP), Airdrie's airfield helped alleviate congestion around Calgary's Lincoln Park airfield.[34]

The Dominion government purchased 640 acres of prairie farmland and immediately converted it into an airport. The facility had three runways forming a triangle (this kept the strong prairie winds from blowing no more than 30 degrees off the centerline of any runway) and two large wooden hangars.

In 1945, the war's end brought with it closure of Air Force flying in Airdrie. Then in 1948, Gordon Bowers purchased the property from Crown Assets for the use of the wartime hangars while the runways fell into a state of disrepair. However, even as the runways slowly deteriorated, they continued to serve student pilots who were now earning their civilian pilot's licenses in nearby Calgary. It also became a location for farmers to base their planes and to load pesticides and chemical fertilizers. This included Airdrie resident Frank Young and his crop spraying company, Skyspray.

By 1957, the abandoned runways were being used as a racetrack for sports car and motorcycle races. Around the same time, Don Southern of the Alberta Trailer Company (ATCO) purchased twenty acres of airfield property. He converted the hangars and offices into commercial facilities for trailer production.

In 1969, Tom Conroy purchased the remaining airport and soon introduced a flying club (known as the Airdrie Country Club of the Air) and fuel services. The Conroy family's contributions turned Airdrie's airport into a friendly base for area pilots. Among the dozens of tenants were the Conroy's own vintage Harvard trainers. These bright yellow planes had served with the Royal Canadian Air Force. With members of the Conroy family at the controls, these planes performed aerobatic feats at numerous local air shows and aviation gatherings.

Tom Conroy passed away in 1979, but his family continued to operate the airport until 1998 when the property was sold to its current owners—Airdrie Airpark Inc. Today, the Airdrie Airport remains a haven for local pilots. Year-round maintenance is offered, allowing planes to fly at night and during Alberta's winter months. Fuel services were reintroduced in the summer of 2005.

FRANK YOUNG, 1958

ATCO FACTORY AT THE
AIRDRIE AIRPORT, CA. 1960s

Glenbow Archives NA-5713-15

## THE JOLLY SHOPPER

*Service with a smile*

Johnnie Loveday ran the Jolly Shopper from the late 1940s until 1969.[35]

Shopping at the Jolly Shopper was somewhat different from strolling down the aisles of today's big-box supermarkets. Customers could phone in their orders and then Johnnie Loveday and his staff would gather up the groceries. It was a time-consuming process but a big part of the business. Orders were placed in whatever crates or boxes that were available—truly recycling! On Saturdays, especially, the boxes would be lined down the aisles ready for pick-up.

Airdrie residents knew Johnnie Loveday as a man with a generous spirit. Many people bought groceries on credit and would pay when they could. Airdrie resident Margaret (Carlson) Fowler recalled paying her grocery bill with eggs!

In addition to running the store, Johnnie Loveday served on the village council between 1953 and 1962. Between 1959 and 1962 he served as village reeve. He retired from the store in 1969 and passed away in 1990.

THE JOLLY SHOPPER, 1964

## Store cat catches cat burglars!

*The store cat often slept on the blue jeans that Dad had for sale. There were several break-ins that I can remember. One time the robbers stole blue jeans and cigarettes. The RCMP noticed the cat and were smart enough to think she could help convict the suspects. They finger (paw) printed her and then matched the prints to ones on the recovered blue jeans. Because of that, the robbers were found guilty.*

Janet (Loveday) Mason
2007

Behind the counter, Johnnie Loveday had countless wooden boxes with order books in them. He'd write your order down and he kept records for all the town people and farmers around. Then at some point you would settle your account.

Dan Oneil
2008

Johnnie carried a lot of people on credit. Many people might have gone hungry if it wasn't for Johnnie.

Elaine McCracken
2008

I remember Mrs. M. Hawkey bringing us a fresh turkey for Christmas to thank Dad for letting her charge her groceries.

As a young child, I spent many hours under a table in the store, reading everything I could find, especially all the comic books. I started working there the summer I turned 13.

Ed and Anne Wright ran the other general store in town. Ed was a school teacher and Anne did most of the store work. They were really good (Loveday family) friends. There was no competition between the stores. There were Wright's customers and there were Johnnie's and everyone was okay with that. When Dad was away, Anne and Ed would help Mom with the butcher shop or anything else she had a problem with. Kind of amazing really!

Janet (Loveday) Mason
2008

JOHNNIE LOVEDAY

# DUSAN'S CLOTHING STORE

*Tailored to measure*

When local farmers, ranchers and oilrig workers needed sturdy clothes, they knew just where to go—Dusan's Clothing Store.[36]

Opened August 1, 1950, Dusan's Clothing Store sold men's, women's and children's wear to the local population. Dusan's slogan was "Tailored to measure, ready to wear, with a complete line of fine footwear." As Airdrie was a village at the time, Dusan's Clothing Store catered mostly to "working folk" by offering blue jeans, coveralls, underwear and socks, as well as rubber boots, work boots and cowboy boots. There was also a selection of business suits and dress shoes. Cowboy hats, hats, sunglasses, Brylcreem™, razors, batteries, watches, radios, clocks, hair clippers, and shoe polish were among other merchandise. Another service Dusan's offered its customers was clothing alterations and shoe repairs.

The store was located in the front of the property, facing Main Street, while Dusan Milutinovic maintained his residence in the back with his wife and seven children. A well-tended vegetable garden spanned the backyard of the entire property. During the winter, a portion of the backyard was flooded to create an ice rink for family skating.

In 1959, Dusan purchased the building next door, which used to be the Post Office. This doubled the size of the store. In the late 1960s, Dusan purchased two more lots to the south, which had formerly housed the Handy Lunch and a confectionery. After connecting the properties, the store was four times the original size. Dusan expanded his product line to include appliances and televisions.

The store continued operation until Dusan Milutinovic retired in 1987. He continued to live there until he sold the property to a local developer in mid-2000 and moved to Calgary.

# WATER TOWER

*In case of emergency, turn tap!*

The water tower has been a familiar landmark in Airdrie since it was built in 1959 to store water for emergencies. At that time, a water and sewage system was also built for the town. Despite the new tower, water pressure was low and almost non-existent in the summer. This was due to the tower being at an inadequate elevation.[37] The water tower was heated at the base during the winter to prevent freezing.

In 1972, a large reservoir was built at the south end of Airdrie, making the tower obsolete. Five years later, the tower was no longer in use. Since then, people have wondered what should become of the empty tower. Options ranged from tearing it down to using it as advertising space. In 2003, the water tower had a new lease on life when council voted unanimously not to tear it down.[38] By September of that year, the tower had a shiny new coat of paint and black letters proudly displaying the city's name.

> The contract for the laying of sewer, water lines, lagoon, etc. was awarded to Borger Bros. at a sum of $67,823.00. The contract calls for the completion by Borger Bros. by the 31st July 1959. The tower will be started in the middle of April, and Borger Bros. will be required to have their part of it completed by this date.
>
> *Rocky View News and Market Examiner*
>
> February 17, 1959

# AIRDRIE PUBLIC LIBRARY

*Imagination, inspiration and information*

The story of the Airdrie Public Library officially began on December 6th, 1971.[39] Since then, the library has enjoyed continued growth and experienced several relocations. First housed in a 4 m × 4.5 m (13' × 15') windowless room, it was initially opened to the public for seven hours a week. Within a year, it had moved to the "little white building" north of the water tower.

During the next five years, the library operated with a rotating staff of about 20 volunteers. The budget was $1700, with the Town providing the building and paying for utilities. It was during this time that the library established its worth to the community. The energetic and dedicated volunteers acquired new materials, painted, decorated and actively promoted the library resources to the community.

Through the 1970s until the first few years of the 2000s, the library grew and moved locations several times. To meet the demands of a growing city, staff was hired, hours extended and thousands of books added to the collection. By March 2006, the library had moved to its present location, just north of the City of Airdrie building.

The Airdrie Public Library is a hub of community activity. In addition to books, programs are offered for all ages and interests. Adults can take part in financial planning and genealogy workshops, while teens and families enjoy hands-on activities.

Through the library's application of new technology plus its membership in the Marigold Library System, Airdrie residents now have access to literally millions of books from across Alberta. The library is working to make information available in many different formats, including e-books, MP3 audio-books and a world languages collection. Thanks to strong community support, the library is sure to be a gathering place for decades to come.

PAUL RABEL AT
THE TOWN AND
COUNTRY CENTRE
LIBRARY,
1978

EARLY 1970s            MID 1990s            2006

# ENVIRONMENTAL EDUCATION CENTRE

*Behind recycled doors*

Taking the lead in the "green revolution" is a big task, but Airdrie's Environmental Education Centre (EEC) is designed for the job.[40] With doors, windows and sinks reused from other sites and solar panels providing heat and electricity, the centre embodies the true meaning of the 3 R's—reduce, reuse and recycle.

Opened in 2002, the EEC is the pride and joy of the City of Airdrie's Environmental Services Department. Education and awareness programs are the cornerstone of the facility. Members of the public and numerous school and community groups, such as Girl Guides and Scouts, have visited the centre and discovered the ins and outs of sustainable living.

The centre incorporates green design and construction ideas from beyond Alberta, such as Australian dual-flush toilets and straw bale walls more typical of the American southwest. In turn, the EEC is an award-winning facility that serves as a model for green living in Canada. In 2007, a delegation from the Federation of Canadian Municipalities visited the centre.[41] The visit offered delegates from across the country the opportunity to see how environmental policies can be put into action on a practical level.

For Airdrie residents, the EEC demonstrates how big and small changes can have a positive impact on the local environment. By taking a leadership role in Alberta and Canada, Airdrie's Environmental Education Centre is putting the city on a path to a sustainable future.

# CITY OF AIRDRIE
*From bylaws to beautification*

For more than 100 years, Airdrie residents have come together to form a body of leadership to run the business of the hamlet, village, town and now city.

Village Council minutes from the 1920s and 1930s indicate that over the years, meetings were held in a variety of locations, including Watson and Stewarts Store, the Union Bank and the Royal Bank of Canada.[42]

By the 1960s, Village Council held its regular meetings in a small Farmers Union of Alberta building on Main Street.[43] In the summer of 1966, the Village opened a new civic centre on the southwest corner of First Avenue North and Bowers Street.[44] This building included council chambers, office space, an R.C.M.P. station and garage.[45]

In 1989, City Hall moved to 125 Main Street. In 2003, City Hall moved to 400 Main Street into a new building redesigned from a grocery store. A total of approximately 171 staff were spread between six different City of Airdrie buildings.

As Airdrie has grown, so too have the number of staff it takes to run the city. In 2008, approximately 260 full time and 120 part-time staff helped to keep the City running smoothly.[46] This number is projected to grow significantly in the coming years.

**By-Law No. 1**

**April 24, 1918**
Moved by Farr seconded Clayton that council see that streets are put into good shape at once.

**May 30, 1919**
Moved by J.R. McCracken that all cattle running at large between 9pm and 7am be impounded.

**April 3, 1927**
The Council of the Village of Airdrie enacts as follows:
1. That it shall be unlawful for any person to allow his horses, cattle, hogs, sheep, or mules to run at large within the village limits at any time of the year.

VILLAGE OFFICE, LATE 1960s

TOWN OF AIRDRIE OFFICE

1974

where the streets
(and communities, parks and schools!)
have historic names...

RJ HAWKEY ELEMENTARY SCHOOL

Farr Cre

Main St

Jensen Dr

Cooper's Crossing

BERT CHURCH HIGH SCHOOL

A number of street, park, school and community names honour Airdrie's pioneer families and local community leaders. While some places are named after local individuals, in many instances, the names honour the families that helped build Airdrie.

McCRACKEN CRES

RALPH McCALL

## A.E. BOWERS ELEMENTARY SCHOOL AND BOWERS STREET

The Bowers name in Airdrie originates with settlers Arthur E. Bowers and his wife Esther Annie (sister of William Croxford). They homesteaded here in 1901, building a barn and Airdrie's first house. Lots for the new hamlet of Airdrie came from portions of the Bowers and Croxford homesteads. A.E. Bowers opened a store and served as postmaster between 1903 and 1907.[47]

In early 1907, the Bowers family moved to the west coast but returned to Airdrie in 1911. At this time, A.E. Bowers purchased farmland upon which the school that bears his name now sits. He also ran a supply store that was later sold to Dr. Edwards. A.E. Bowers passed away in an automobile accident in July of 1922.[48]

THE BOWERS FAMILY, 1906

## BERT CHURCH HIGH SCHOOL AND BERT CHURCH *LIVE* THEATRE

Bert Church was a Balzac rancher who raised purebred Hereford cattle. He was a member of the Calgary Rural School Board between 1951 and 1964. He served as chairman for the last 10 years of that term. The school board worked to secure Airdrie's first high school with George McDougall High School opening in 1963.[49] Bert Church was an active member of the Balzac community—involved with the Balzac Seed Cleaning Plant, Rockyview Planning Commission and 4-H.

## BOWEN PARK

Bowen Park is located in the community of Reunion. The park is named after the Bowen family, who began farming in this area in the 1930s.[50] In addition to the park's name, plaques and a bronze statue in the park honour the Bowen family.[51]

## COOPER'S CROSSING

GEORGE AND ELEANOR COOPER

The Cooper family arrived in this area in 1892, looking for good land. They found it in Airdrie, and so began a family legacy in grain farming that lasted more than a century. Born during the very first Calgary Stampede in 1912, George Cooper together with his wife Eleanor, farmed this land and prospered. They dedicated themselves to a lifetime of community service.[52]

## CROXFORD PLACE

Land owned by the Croxford family became lots for the hamlet of Airdrie. Their house was the second dwelling built in Airdrie.[53] In 1902 or 1903, Dan McDonald moved a building onto the Croxford homestead and it

THE CROXFORD FAMILY HOME

became the hotel (the Old Hotel). Croxford land also became home to Airdrie's first church built in 1903. That same year, Mr. and Mrs. Thomas Croxford (parents of William Croxford and Esther Annie [Croxford] Bowers) arrived in Airdrie from west of Irricana.

THE THOMAS CROXFORD FAMILY

## ÉCOLE EDWARDS ELEMENTARY SCHOOL

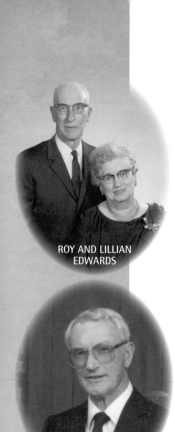

ROY AND LILLIAN
EDWARDS

Members of the Edwards family have played an active role in the community since Airdrie first became a village. Dr. W.F. Edwards served as Airdrie's doctor for 33 years, from 1907 to 1940. Roy Edwards (brother of Dr. Edwards) and his wife Lillian were teachers in the district for many years. Roy also operated a pool hall and barber shop.[54] In 1910, Dr. Edwards' sister, Nellie Pole, arrived in Airdrie. She also contributed to education in Airdrie, was active in the Airdrie United Church and worked on the One Day's Journey book project.

## EDWARDS WAY

Bob Edwards (son of Roy and Lillian Edwards) served on village council between 1962 and 1971, including seven years as reeve.[55,56] He drove a school bus for many years and was an active member of Airdrie United Church.

BOB EDWARDS

## FARR CRESCENT

The Farr and Jenkins store was part of Airdrie's original building boom in the early 1900s. At this time, Art Farr was responsible for hauling mail between the post office and the train. In 1907, Les Farr had the contract to erect telephone lines in the area for Alberta Government Telephones.[57] The Farr and Jenkins store housed the telephone exchange. Les Farr served on village council, including time as secretary-treasurer and reeve between 1915 and 1918.[58]

LES FARR AND
MURIEL Van SICKLE, 1928

TOM AND NANCY FARR FAMILY, CA. 1940s

LAFE VAN SICKLE AND
ART FARR, 1904

## FLETT DRIVE/PLACE/CRESCENT

Thomas Flett and son were among the first of Airdrie's blacksmiths. In the late 1910s until the mid 1920s, Lloyd Flett served on village council, including time as reeve.[59] The Fletts purchased a home in Airdrie from the Bushfield family in 1917. They lived in this home until 1964.[60] The house now stands in Heritage Park Historical Village in Calgary and represents a typical early 1900s home in western Canada. Dale Flett was five-time Rangeland Derby Chuckwagon champion at the Calgary Stampede in the late 1950s and early 1960s.[61]

## FLETCHER PARK AND FLETCHER ROAD

In 1903, Mr. and Mrs. Thomas Fletcher and Mary Fletcher were charter members of Airdrie Methodist Church.[62] Between the 1920s and the late 1930s, Ed Fletcher ran a dray and horse team, taking the mail from the train drop-off point to the post office. Later Lloyd Fletcher and Allen Fletcher ran the mail.[63] In the early 1960s, Ruth Fletcher was one of the town women on standby to receive calls on the fire phone and sound the siren to alert volunteer firefighters.[64] In the 21st century, a sixth generation of Fletchers still calls the Airdrie area home.

ED FLETCHER

## HAWKEY CRESCENT

Members of the Hawkey family were among the earliest settlers in the hamlet of Airdrie. R.L. Hawkey (father of Lillian Edwards) was a devout Methodist and served as a lay preacher in the church.[65] During 1903 or 1904, Luther Hawkey built a two-storey building on today's First Avenue North, just east of Main Street.[66] With shops on ground level, the second storey had a large room that served as a community hall. Church services, meetings and dances occurred here on a regular basis. Frank Hawkey was involved with road building in the 1910s and 1920s.[67]

FRANK AND MARIANNE HAWKEY FAMILY, 1934

ANNIE AND ROBERT LUTHER HAWKEY

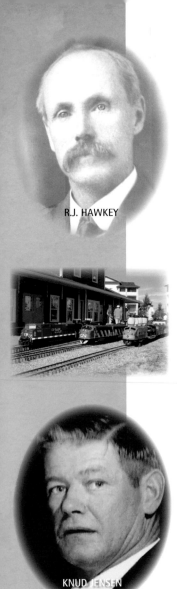

## R.J. HAWKEY ELEMENTARY SCHOOL

In 1904, Airdrie's first schoolhouse opened with Robert John Hawkey as teacher. He taught there for nine years before moving to teach in Cochrane, Elnora and Glen Rock.[68] In 1918, he returned to Airdrie to open the village's first bakery.[69] He later went back to teaching, but then moved on to village politics, serving as reeve between 1933 and 1942. R.J. Hawkey also ran a dairy and was secretary-treasurer of the school. He was involved with Airdrie United Church as a treasurer, superintendent of Sunday school and choir member.[70] Descendents of R.J. Hawkey still reside in the Airdrie area.

R.J. HAWKEY

## IRON HORSE PARK

The term Iron Horse is an old-fashioned name for a railway locomotive. Iron Horse Park pays tribute to the early days of railway in western Canada.[71] The park includes a miniature train that kids of all ages can enjoy!

## JENSEN PARK AND COMMUNITY OF JENSEN

In 1930, the Jensen family left their native Denmark and headed for Alberta.[72] In 1936, Knud Jensen returned to Denmark and married Lilly Sorensen. The newlyweds traveled back across the ocean to settle into married life in Airdrie. In 1938, the Jensens purchased a farm from Dr. Edwards. Here, they grew grain and raised cows. By the mid-1940s, Knud Jensen was active as a village councillor, serving as reeve between 1950 and 1959. He passed away in 1965 at the age of 49 years. In 1999, the Airdrie Over 50 Club recognized Lilly Jensen for her community volunteer work. Generations of Jensens continue to reside in the Airdrie area.

KNUD JENSEN

LILLY JENSEN

## KING'S HEIGHTS

One possible meaning of the Scottish word "Airdrie" is the "King's Heights."[73] A unique feature of Airdrie is its elevation makes it one of the highest cities in Canada.

## McCRACKEN CRESCENT

Anna McCracken married Dr. W.F. Edwards in 1908. Politics must run in the McCracken blood, as several generations have taken their turn on local council. J.R. McCracken served on village council between the 1910s and 1930s, including time as reeve.[74] During the 1960s, Norman McCracken served as secretary-treasurer of the village.[75] Between 1984 and 1986, Elaine McCracken took her turn, serving on town council and then city council.[76]

LULU AND JIM McCRACKEN

## MARTIN McKEE BRIDGE

In 1981, Martin McKee moved with his family from Northern Ireland to Alberta.[77,78] They were accidental arrivals to the city, first looking for houses in Calgary but choosing to settle in Airdrie. By 1987, Martin McKee had established McKee Homes Ltd. and was building homes that would help shape the look and feel of Airdrie. He was an active member of the community, becoming involved with the Airdrie United Church and the Rotary Club.

MARTIN McKEE

## MONKLANDS SOCCER PARK

The word Monklands refers to an area in Scotland made up of the burghs (towns) of Airdrie and Coatsbridge. The name itself is very old, first recorded in 1323; however, monks were living and farming in that area of Scotland in 1162.[79]

## MORRIS PLACE/CRESCENT

These streets are named after the Morris family. Gordon Morris signed up for service during World War II. He operated Airdrie's first gas station on Highway No. 2.[80] Gordon also served on village council from 1965 to 1971.[81] Jim Morris did carpentry and painting, and was the Airdrie United Church custodian for many years.[82] Spence Morris was a school bus driver and longtime custodian at George McDougall High School.[83] He was also a volunteer on the Police Commission.

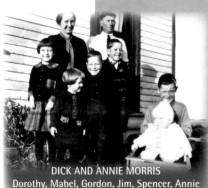
DICK AND ANNIE MORRIS
Dorothy, Mabel, Gordon, Jim, Spencer, Annie

MURIEL CLAYTON

RALPH McCALL

TED LORD

## MURIEL CLAYTON MIDDLE SCHOOL

This school is named to honour the first teacher in the Airdrie District. Emily Muriel Mason was born in England in 1882.[84] With her family, she immigrated to Chicago in 1891, where she lived for eight years and completed her education. Miss Mason became the first teacher of Sunnyside School when it opened its door on February 22, 1899 to nine students. The Sunnyside School was located on the same property as the Dickson Stopping House (along the highway between Airdrie and Crossfield). In 1904, Muriel married rancher Jack Clayton and together they had 11 children.

## RALPH McCALL SCHOOL

Ralph McCall spent 21 years as a teacher at both George McDougall and Bert Church High Schools.[85] He was also Airdrie's deputy mayor from 1977 until his retirement in 1989. Ralph McCall is remembered for his love of the community, history, gardening, singing and devotion to his family.

## TED LORD MEMORIAL PARK

Between 1948 and 1989, Ted Lord owned and operated the Banff Trail Nurseries. He was the founder and first president of the Landscape Alberta Nursery Trades Association (LANTA).[86] In 1981, he was named an Airdrie Citizen of the Year. He was also involved with the Airdrie Lions Club and Airdrie United Church. The community of Waterstone sits on the former Lord nursery.

## COMMUNITY OF THORBURN

The Thorburn family arrived in Calgary in 1899, and in 1903 they settled in Airdrie.[87] The following year, Margaret and Douglas Thorburn were among the first students to attend the new Airdrie School.[88] In 1905, Robert Thorburn established a hardware store on land that was once part of the Croxford homestead, only to have it burn down two years later.[89] James Thorburn ran the meat market between the late 1910s and 1925.[90] In 1923, James Thorburn was on village council, and in 1925 he served as reeve.[91]

J.A. THORNBURN

## VETERANS BOULEVARD

Named in 2005, Canada's Year of the Veteran, this road honours the local men and women who served our country during World War I and World War II.[92,93] Airdrie and area residents have a history of signing up for service, participating in many wars and conflicts, including the Riel Rebellion, World War I, World War II, Somalia, Kosovo and Afghanistan.

## WILLIAMSTOWN

Born in Ontario to Scottish parents, Sir William Mackenzie was one of Canada's great entrepreneurs of the early twentieth century. Responsible for the development of the Calgary and Edmonton Railway, he also laid the foundation for other familiar enterprises, including the Canadian National Railway and the Toronto Transit Commission.[94]

## YANKEE VALLEY BOULEVARD

Many of Airdrie's earliest settlers arrived here from Ontario. However, around 1906, a group of American settlers began making their way to the area.[95] Homesteaders began to refer to the area as Yankee Valley, and the name stuck!

clubs, organizations and societies

Airdrie's clubs, organizations and societies offer local residents the opportunity to build a strong sense of community, as well as enjoy time for recreation and socialization. These clubs depend on the enthusiasm, dedication and support of volunteers. Whether engaging youth, building friendships, encouraging fitness or supporting local charities, dozens upon dozens of local clubs help reveal Airdrie's community spirit in all that they do. [96]

## Rockyview Art Club — Artist Guild of Airdrie

Members of the Airdrie Artist Guild have been sharing a love of art since the Guild was first established in 1988. The Guild displays its artistic creations at community venues, including the Airdrie Public Library and Smitty's Restaurant. These artworks make a colourful addition to the city, while revealing some of Airdrie's talented people, special places and moments in time.

CORY HABBERFIELD AND HIS 4-H WINNING COW
ARTIST: TAMI HORT

COOPER'S CROSSING PARKLAND
ARTIST: VERONIKA CINDRIC

HEAVY HORSE AT THE AIRDRIE CANADA DAY PARADE
ARTIST: WENDY BROWNLEE

# Airdrie Regional ARTS Society

## Airdrie Regional ARTS Society

ARTS envisions itself as making arts-related resources and facilities accessible to people throughout the region. ARTS is also committed to fostering, supporting and promoting artistic pursuits that everyone can enjoy. By running workshops and educational events, ARTS is securing its place as a leader in the Airdrie arts community.

ARR AND JENKINS GENERAL STORE.

OLD AIRDRIE
ARTIST: JANE ROMANISHKO

The Airdrie Regional ARTS Society participated in the 2008 Airdrie Empty Bowls for Hunger Arts Festival. Money raised during the festival helps support the Airdrie Food Bank.

ARTS
Airdrie Regional ARTS Society

001

DATE 2008/07/08
YYYY MM DD

PAY TO THE ORDER OF  AIRDRIE FOOD BANK xx 7000

SEVEN THOUSAND DOLLARS

ARTS Auction

# The Bert Church *Live* Theatre

## The Bert Church *Live* Theatre

Since opening in 1984, the Bert Church Live Theatre has hosted a real cast of characters and productions—from amateur theatre groups to big-name musical acts. It has become a vital part of the city, connecting audiences to engaging and entertaining performances.

AIRDRIE LITTLE THEATRE CAST MEMBERS

## Airdrie Community Choir

Members of the Airdrie Community Choir have been raising their voices in song since the group formed in 1985. By performing at a variety of local events, the Airdrie Community Choir has become an integral part of the community and the local performing arts scene.

1985/1986

2007/2008

## Royal Canadian Legion and Auxiliary – Airdrie Branch

The Airdrie Legion works to preserve the memory of fallen soldiers and supports local war veterans. The Legion's work in the community ensures that the sacrifice these soldiers have made in serving their country is never forgotten. Members of the Ladies Auxiliary include women directly involved with the service and the female relatives of Legion members. Over the years, these women have worked hard to support the Legion and the Airdrie community, sponsoring bazaars, fashion shows, lunches, bake sales and poppy sales.

## Airdrie and District Rotary Club

Airdrie and District Rotary Club is actively involved with a variety of local projects, including Rotary Youth Enrichment Program, the Rotary Youth Leadership Awards program, the Miss School Miss Out program, and the Youth Exchange program, among others.

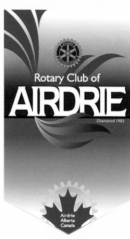

AIRDRIE KINSMEN CLUB, 2005

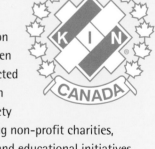

## Kinsmen Club of Airdrie

Since it was chartered on May 9, 1981, the Kinsmen Club of Airdrie has injected more than half a million dollars into a wide variety of local causes, including non-profit charities, clubs, school bursaries and educational initiatives, school playgrounds, youth groups, sporting teams, institutions and individuals in need.

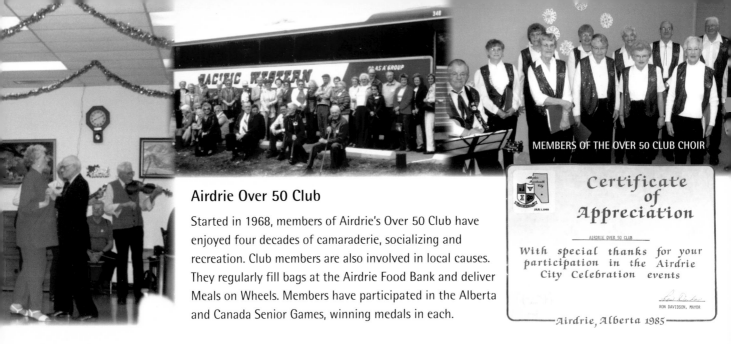

MEMBERS OF THE OVER 50 CLUB CHOIR

## Airdrie Over 50 Club

Started in 1968, members of Airdrie's Over 50 Club have enjoyed four decades of camaraderie, socializing and recreation. Club members are also involved in local causes. They regularly fill bags at the Airdrie Food Bank and deliver Meals on Wheels. Members have participated in the Alberta and Canada Senior Games, winning medals in each.

Certificate of Appreciation

AIRDRIE OVER 50 CLUB

With special thanks for your participation in the Airdrie City Celebration events

RON DAVIDSON, MAYOR

Airdrie, Alberta 1985

## Wild Rose Shriners Club

Members of the Wild Rose Shriners Club are committed to helping sick children get the medical care they need. This club is responsible for the Shriners Child Care Coach, which transports sick children and their families to local hospitals and Shriners hospitals in the United States.

## Nose Creek Historical Society

The Nose Creek Historical Society began in 1960 with the production of a published account of local family histories. Over the years, they have sponsored various activities to commemorate significant historical events, starting in 1972 with the unveiling of a cairn honouring the Canadian Militia and the RCMP and ending in 2003 with a tribute to music in the community. In 2004, they began marking the locations of local one-roomed schools with plaques mounted on rock cairns. The goal of the society is to preserve the history of the Nose Creek Valley and area.

Nose Creek Historical Society executive at the dedication of the Columbia School in 2007. (L-R) Harold Watters, Brenda Watters, Dorothy Pedersen, Kathy Shuttleworth, Valerie Jobson, Grant Shuttleworth, Larry Bilben.

## Airdrie Chamber of Commerce

The first Airdrie Chamber of Commerce formed in 1957 but was dissolved in 1961, due to declining membership. In 1973, a new Chamber of Commerce was organized. The Chamber was a founding supporter of the Airdrie Hire-a-Student office, an evening sponsor of the Airdrie Festival of Lights and for over 12 years has sponsored the Calgary Philharmonic Orchestra Community Concert held annually at the Bert Church Live Theatre. In January 2009, the Chamber of Commerce welcomed their 400th member and membership continues to increase as Airdrie grows.[97]

AIRDRIE CHAMBER OF COMMERCE CELEBRATES ITS 25th ANNIVERSARY, 1998

AIRDRIE
Chamber of Commerce

## Airdrie Girl Guides

Guiding in Airdrie began in 1974, with a 15-member Brownie Pack. By 1990, Airdrie offered a full range of Guiding opportunities for all ages, including Sparks, Brownies, Girl Guides, Pathfinders and Rangers. Through service to community, Guiders learn how to help others. Airdrie Guiders have contributed to the Over 50 Club, performed at the Bethany Care Centre, helped at the Festival of Lights, filled Christmas shoeboxes, helped at Inn from the Cold, and sold daffodils for the Cancer Society.

## Airdrie Scouts

Airdrie's Scout history begins in the early part of the 1900s with a troop led by the village blacksmith, William MacKay. In 1948, L.R. Blair organized another local troop that continued on until 1951. Today, Airdrie has a number of Scout groups. Members of the Airdrie Scouts are active in the community through programs such as Pitch-in Canada—a springtime cleanup of alleyways, parks and creek beds. Each year, Airdrie Scouts take part in local Remembrance Day services. The Scouts also participate in the annual Airdrie Kub Kar Rally. From small blocks of wood, Scouts are challenged to build a small racing vehicle—some innovative creations find their way onto the mini-speedway!

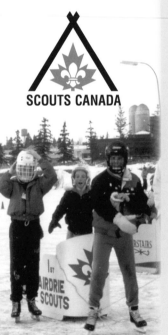

AIRDRIE HELPING HANDS 4-H MULTI CLUB PUBLIC SPEAKING EVENT, 2008

## Airdrie 4-H

The first 4-H club in Airdrie was the Airdrie Junior Grain Club started in 1938 with Howard Wright, a local farmer and seed grower, as leader. There were 25 members—all boys. This club disbanded in 1941 due to 14 members enlisting in the armed services. Organized in March 1950, the Airdrie 4-H Beef Club began with 30 boys and girls, 11 of which still live in the Airdrie area today. There have been several other 4-H clubs in the Airdrie district, including gardening, sewing, horses, sheep and swine. Currently, there is the Airdrie 4-H Beef Club, the Airdrie Flying Hooves 4-H Club (horses), the Midnight Express Light Horse 4-H Club, the Airdrie Helping Hands 4-H Multi Club and the Golden Rod 4-H Multi Club, both non-livestock clubs.

4-H stands for Head, Heart, Health and Hands

MARJORIE CLAYTON, CA. 1950s

## Airdrie Horticultural Society

Since forming in 2001, the Airdrie Horticultural Society has been the "place to meet" for Airdrie residents with green-thumbs and those with green-thumb aspirations. With close to 100 members, gardeners enjoy the opportunity to share and discuss gardening tips, listen to guest speakers and engage in hands-on workshops. The society coordinates several community projects, including the Community Garden, which is located in the southwest corner of Monklands Soccer Park.

## Airdrie and District Agricultural Society

Although Airdrie has recently grown into a truly urban centre, it maintains a strong rural connection. Since forming in 1974, the Airdrie and District Agricultural Society has worked to promote agriculture and related activities in the community. The Society depends on a team of dedicated volunteers, including some of the founding members who remain active on the Board today. Members support a wide variety of programs related to youth, education, agriculture, sports and community building. The Society hosts, organizes and funds the Airdrie and District Annual Fall Fair. Exhibits are judged in a number of categories, including artwork, handicrafts, flowers, vegetables, woodworking and more.

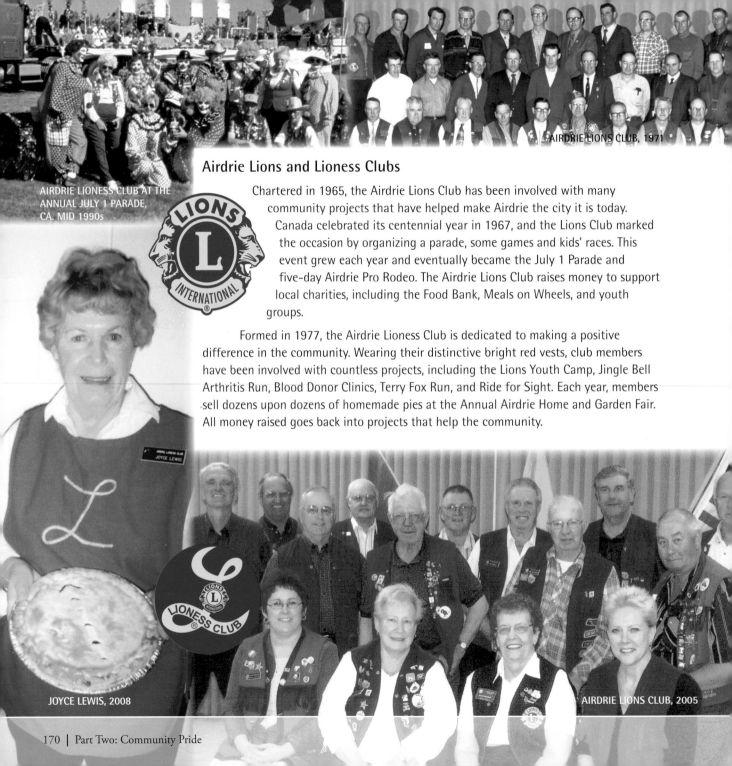

AIRDRIE LIONS CLUB, 1971

AIRDRIE LIONESS CLUB AT THE
ANNUAL JULY 1 PARADE,
CA. MID 1990s

## Airdrie Lions and Lioness Clubs

Chartered in 1965, the Airdrie Lions Club has been involved with many community projects that have helped make Airdrie the city it is today. Canada celebrated its centennial year in 1967, and the Lions Club marked the occasion by organizing a parade, some games and kids' races. This event grew each year and eventually became the July 1 Parade and five-day Airdrie Pro Rodeo. The Airdrie Lions Club raises money to support local charities, including the Food Bank, Meals on Wheels, and youth groups.

Formed in 1977, the Airdrie Lioness Club is dedicated to making a positive difference in the community. Wearing their distinctive bright red vests, club members have been involved with countless projects, including the Lions Youth Camp, Jingle Bell Arthritis Run, Blood Donor Clinics, Terry Fox Run, and Ride for Sight. Each year, members sell dozens upon dozens of homemade pies at the Annual Airdrie Home and Garden Fair. All money raised goes back into projects that help the community.

JOYCE LEWIS, 2008

AIRDRIE LIONS CLUB, 2005

# AIRDRIE RODEO RANCH

## Airdrie Rodeo Ranch Association

Western heritage is alive and well in Airdrie, thanks in part to the Airdrie Rodeo Ranch Association. Held in 1967, the Airdrie Lions Club sponsored Airdrie's first rodeo as a one-day event. The rodeo became an annual event successfully expanding with each passing year. Formed in 1986, the Airdrie Rodeo Ranch Association took over hosting the rodeo from the Airdrie Lions Club. The Airdrie Pro Rodeo is 100% volunteer-driven and depends on more than 200 volunteers to stage the event. The rodeo continues to grow each year with the addition of new events, such as concerts, ranch hand competitions and "Tough Enough to Wear Pink" promotions run in support of the Canadian Breast Cancer Foundation.

# SPORTS CLUBS

Sports have always been an important part of life in Airdrie. Early settlers brought with them a love of baseball and hockey. Men and women, young and old, enjoyed taking part in sports for fun and competition.

Sporting events were a time for rural dwellers to socialize in the village. Sports Days were a great opportunity for people to come together in friendly competition and then end the day with a dance. These events often made newspaper headlines. The news reports included detailed descriptions of who played, the outcome of the game, who attended and who didn't attend!

Formed in 1907, Airdrie's first hockey team played according to "Ontario rules," with seven players on each team.[98] The team traveled to nearby communities, such as Didsbury, Crossfield and Calgary. Many of the people who played hockey in winter played baseball in summer.

The Airdrie Tennis Club was going strong in the 1920s. A notice by the club in a 1922 edition of the Airdrie Recorder newspaper declared "everybody plays tennis."[99]

In the 1940s, horse races were held on a track where the Plainsmen Arena now sits. The Airdrie Curling Club was formed in 1944, and many local old-timers recall their mothers and sisters curling in long skirts!

Today, Airdrie residents enjoy sports of all sorts. Old favourites, such as hockey and curling, are still very popular, while additional favourites, such as soccer and BMX, attract more participants each year.

GIRLS DRILL PRACTICE, 1928

AIRDRIE OLDTIMERS HOCKEY TEAM, CA. 1970s

AIRDRIE ICE HOCKEY TEAM, 1928-1929

## Airdrie Hockey

For more than 100 years, local residents have enjoyed playing in their own version of "Hockey Night in Airdrie." Whether practicing "shots on goal" in a backyard rink or skating towards making it in the "big league," there's no doubt that Airdrie loves hockey. Today, local hockey associations include Adult Hockey, Airdrie Minor Hockey Association, Airdrie Thunder, and Oldtimers Hockey. Hockey's "cousin," ringette, is also popular in the city and is organized through the Airdrie Ringette Association.

AIRDRIE ICE HOCKEY TEAM, MID 1930s

# AIRDRIE

## 𝒜
### LITTLE LEAGUE BASEBALL

## Airdrie Baseball and Softball

For nearly a century, Airdrie residents have enjoyed playing ballgames. Today, Airdrie offers players a variety of leagues to choose from, including Airdrie Girls Softball Association, Ladies Recreational Fastball, Mixed Industrial Slo-pitch, Men's Slo-pitch and Airdrie Little League Baseball.

AIRDRIE BASEBALL TEAM, 1928

AIRDRIE BASEBALL TEAM, DATE UNKNOWN

Curling in those early days was certainly different from today. The brooms were much like household brooms with long bristles and the women wore long skirts! Everybody had to buy their own rocks!

2008

2008

## Airdrie Curling Club

With a steady hand and precision timing, members of the Airdrie Curling Club have enjoyed making a clean sweep of curling for more than 60 years. The club's history began in 1944 when curlers brought their own rocks and played on an outdoor rink. The following year, the club moved to a building on the corner of First Avenue and First Street, near where the post office now sits. In 1979, the club moved into the Town and Country Centre. Run as a volunteer organization, the club revolves around building friendships, skills and sportsmanship in curlers of all ages.

CURLERS TOM FARR, W. CLAPPERTON, E.B. DEWITT AND WALTER MOEN AT THE GOLDEN JUBILEE BONSPIEL IN CALGARY, 1954      Glenbow Archives NA-5600-7330b

Part Three

*opportunity for the future*

Airdrie — the next 100 years

Airdrie has always been a city of opportunity—a place where people can grow a business, raise a family and enjoy small-city living. Opportunity for the future will focus on Airdrie's pioneering role as a leader in sustainability. Airdrie's future will be driven by a youthful energy that prides itself on innovation and adaptability.

# LOOKING BACK...LOOKING FORWARD

More than one hundred years ago in 1906, Airdrie's school teacher, Mr. R. J. Hawkey, put on a concert along with a box social to raise money for "extras" for the school. Part of the program was the reading of essays written on the topic of "the world fifty years from now."

Inspired by this task, in 2008 grade five students from Ecole Airdrie, Meadowbrook, Muriel Clayton, Our Lady of Peace and Ralph McCall Middle School were asked to predict "the next 100 years for Airdrie." Their predictions offer some insight as to where the city might be headed...

*Airdrie will be connected with Calgary.*

*...future population will be about 500,000...*
*...future population over 1,000,000...*
*...population of 100,000...*

*As Airdrie grows ...there are more jobs, then the quiet farms might be changed to a busy place with big house, malls, outlets and offices.*

*...I worry about environmental problems like urban sprawl and global warming...Instead of our city taking away all the farmland, houses and buildings will begin to be built upwards instead of outwards. And people won't travel as far to work anymore because they will be able to do most of their work at home with computers and other technologies.*

All the farms will be sold and factories will be put in their place.

...lots of people will grow gardens...

...electricity will be generated by giant wind powered generators.

Solar panels everywhere.

...have an Airdrie Tower...

...have a humongous theme park...

...have own NHL team...

To travel to Calgary and other places, people in Airdrie will travel on bullet trains.

...solar powered cars...

Cars that run on garbage.

...high speed train that will take us to Calgary.

...will be so high tech that ...your car would form around you.

Instead of gas stations there will be battery recharging stations.

Computers will be as thin as a picture book...

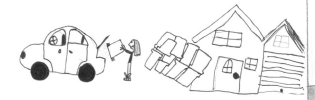

## TAKING STEPS FORWARD...NATURALLY

In just 100 years, Airdrie has gone from a dusty prairie village to one of Canada's fastest growing cities. Airdrie's next 100 years are sure to be just as impressive as more people and businesses begin to call Airdrie home. What makes Airdrie's future so exciting is that innovative environmental programs and projects are putting the city on a path to sustainability.

The City of Airdrie was selected to participate in The Natural Step Canada Program to develop a community sustainability plan.[1] This program will work to reduce Airdrie's ecological footprint. It gives people the tools they need to make decisions that are socially, environmentally and economically sustainable. The future is filled with a feeling of opportunity and optimism balanced with a respect for the environment.

Glenbow Archives NA-2547-10

## INSPIRED BY THE PAST, DESIGNED FOR THE FUTURE

Airdrie's Main Street has been the commercial and social hub of the community for more than 100 years. The downtown streetscape is set to be transformed in the coming years. Development will include the construction of new buildings and the redevelopment of existing structures. The design of new buildings will have a distinct modern style but will reflect ideas firmly rooted in a pioneer past. Storefronts with residential dwellings above were typical of Airdrie's early Main Street. New construction will embrace this mixed-use. By returning to this type of development, people will once again live, work and play right in the heart of Airdrie.[2]

## THE FUTURE LOOKS BRIGHT!

As Airdrie reflects on 100 years of history, it is clear that the city has come a long way in a very short time. From humble railway beginnings, Airdrie has become a vibrant city built on a pioneer spirit, community pride and opportunity for the future. Airdrie's people have made the city what it is today. Airdrie embarks on its next 100 years of history with a true sense of where it has come from and where it is headed. The opportunities and the possibilities are truly endless!

Airdrie milestones

## 1891
Railway station house built

## 1900
First post office built

## 1901
First house built

## 1904
Airdrie's first bank opened by the Union Bank of Canada

## 1900s–1930s
Several blacksmith shops serve Airdrie and area.

## 1907–1940
Dr. W.F. Edwards serves as the country doctor for Airdrie and area.

## 1909
Airdrie proclaimed a village.

## 1909–1910
T. Vincent is Reeve.

## 1911
James Coombes is Reeve.

## 1912
J. Fletcher is Reeve.

## 1913
A.E. Bowers is Reeve.

## 1914
J.R. Laycock is Reeve.

## 1915–1918
Leslie Farr is Reeve.

## 1918/1919
The Spanish influenza epidemic strikes Airdrie. The Old Hotel becomes a makeshift hospital. In Airdrie, four flu-related deaths were reported.

EPIDEMIC INFLUENZA (SPANISH)
This Disease is Highly Communicable. It May Develop Into a Severe Pneumonia.

## 1919–1920
Lloyd Flett is Reeve.

## 1921
The *Airdrie Recorder* newspaper begins publishing.

## 1921–1922
Joseph J. Stewart is Reeve.

## 1922
Dedication of Airdrie United Church. The building still stands today and is one of a handful of historic buildings remaining in the city.

## 1923–1924
J.R. McCracken is Reeve.

## 1925
James Thorburn is Reeve.

## 1926
William R. Jenkins is Reeve.

## 1927–1933
Lafayette Van Sickle is Reeve.

## 1928
Airdrie council grants Calgary Power Ltd. the contract to supply Airdrie with lights and power.

## 1929
First Alberta Wheat Pool elevator built in Airdrie.

## 1932-1962
Mrs. Inez Clayton serves as Airdrie's telephone switchboard operator.

## 1933–1942
R.J. Hawkey is Reeve.

## 1943
Airdrie C.P.R. station burns down.

**1943–1945**
Nat Clogg is Reeve.

**1946–1949**
Sim Meyer is Reeve.

**1950–1958**
Knud Jensen is Reeve.

**1950s**
Closure of the last of the local rural schools with students bused to Airdrie.

**1959**
Water tower built, becoming a prominent landmark feature on the prairie landscape.

**1959–1962**
John Loveday is Reeve.

**1962**
Airdrie receives automatic telephone service.

**1963–1970**
Robert T. Edwards is Reeve.

**1967**
Airdrie hosts its first Foothills Cowboy Association rodeo. In 1994, the rodeo becomes part of the professional rodeo circuit.

**1970–1972**
Major road construction takes place, including the Highway 567 northern overpass, the Yankee Valley underpass, the Balzac overpass and the six-lane Highway 2 (now the QE II Highway).

**1971**
Walter Moen is Reeve. Locals often referred to Reeve Moen as Mayor Moen.

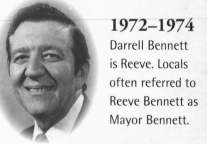

**1972–1974**
Darrell Bennett is Reeve. Locals often referred to Reeve Bennett as Mayor Bennett.

**1974**
Airdrie is proclaimed a town.

**1975–1983**
Darrell Bennett is Mayor.

**1975**
The *Airdrie Echo* begins printing.

## 1984
The 400-seat Bert Church Live Theatre opens.

## 1984
The Dickson-Stevenson Stopping House rest area is opened north of Airdrie. The site is named after a stopping house built on the Calgary Trail in the 1880s—first owned by John Dickson and later Johnston Stevenson.

## 1984-1986
Ron Davidson is Mayor.

## 1985
The self-contained passenger Dayliner train makes its last run between Calgary and Edmonton.

## 1985
Airdrie is proclaimed a city.

## 1986
Airdrie and area experiences a "whopper" of a snowstorm. Nearly 30 cm (12 inches) of snow falls, stranding people for two days. Stephanie Harris was born at home during the storm.

## 1986–1992
Grant McLean is Mayor.

## 1987
Rick Hansen's Man in Motion Tour rolls into Airdrie. Mr. Hansen spoke to a local audience about the abilities of the physically challenged. Local service clubs and schools presented Mr. Hansen with a donation for $13,000.

## 1988
Calgary hosts the XV Olympic Winter Games. 15,000–20,000 residents come out to celebrate the arrival of the Olympic torch relay through Airdrie. The Russian hockey team practices in Airdrie.

## 1988
Nose Creek Valley Museum opens.

## 1990
Palliser Furniture Ltd suffers a devastating fire that burns for days. The company rebuilds, but closes down its Airdrie operation in 2007.

## 1992
The City of Airdrie introduces garbage bag limits along with an extensive recycling program. Airdrie moves towards introducing more sustainability programs and projects.

**1992–2004**
Dan Oneil is Mayor.

## 1995
Airdrie is twinned with Yuto-Cho, Japan.

## 1996
Airdrie Festival of Lights brightens up the holiday season. The festival is considered western Canada's largest, free outdoor light show.

## 1997
Airdrie is twinned with Gwacheon, South Korea. The twinning program provides opportunities for Airdrie and area residents to share cultural experiences, develop friendships and explore economic opportunities.

## 2001
The City of Airdrie opens the Environmental Education Centre highlighting sustainable construction and materials.

## 2004
Linda Bruce is elected to become Airdrie's first female mayor.

## 2004
The newly redeveloped East Lake Recreation and Wellness Centre opens its doors.

## 2007
Airdrie goes live on the air with "The Range" radio station.

## 2007
Totem poles from sister city Gwacheon, South Korea, are erected in Nose Creek Park to celebrate 10 years of twinning.

## 2008
The East Lake Recreation and Wellness Centre is renamed Genesis Place.

## 2009
Airdrie plans to host Alberta's 55 Plus Summer Games with more than 1,000 participants in attendance.

## 2009
A year of celebration for Airdrie's centennial. Many community events are planned to mark the occasion.

# Airdrie's population growth

| YEAR | POPULATION |
|------|------------|
| 1913 | 135 |
| 1914 | 100 |
| 1915 | 135 |
| 1916 | 150 |
| 1917 | 150 |
| 1918 | 160 |
| 1919 | 160 |
| 1920 | 150 |
| 1921 | 150 |
| 1922 | 150 |
| 1923 | 250 |
| 1924 | 150 |
| 1925 | 150 |
| 1926 | 150 |
| 1927 | 150 |
| 1928 | 150 |
| 1929 | - |
| 1930 | 160 |
| 1931 | 160 |
| 1932 | 160 |
| 1933 | 160 |
| 1934 | 160 |
| 1935 | 150 |
| 1936 | 214 |
| 1937 | 150 |
| 1938 | 160 |
| 1939 | 160 |
| 1940 | 160 |
| 1941 | 185 |
| 1942 | 185 |
| 1943 | 180 |
| 1944 | 180 |

| YEAR | POPULATION |
|------|------------|
| 1945 | 200 |
| 1946 | 195 |
| 1947 | 198 |
| 1948 | 255 |
| 1949 | 270 |
| 1950 | 295 |
| 1951 | 267 |
| 1952 | 267 |
| 1953 | 287 |
| 1954 | 287 |
| 1955 | 287 |
| 1956 | 327 |
| 1957 | 327 |
| 1958 | 331 |
| 1959 | 331 |
| 1960 | 400 |
| 1961 | 509 |
| 1962 | 611 |
| 1963 | 679 |
| 1964 | 679 |
| 1965 | 721 |
| 1966 | 795 |
| 1967 | 800 |
| 1968 | 850 |
| 1969 | 948 |
| 1970 | 960 |
| 1971 | 1090 |
| 1972 | 1160 |
| 1973 | 1200 |
| 1974 | 1294 |
| 1975 | 1383 |
| 1976 | 1408 |

| YEAR | POPULATION |
|------|------------|
| 1977 | 1442 |
| 1978 | 2248 |
| 1979 | 3879 |
| 1980 | 5897 |
| 1981 | 8265 |
| 1982 | 9981 |
| 1983 | 10431 |
| 1984 | 10264 |
| 1985* | 10349 |
| 1986 | 10434 |
| 1987* | 10696 |
| 1988 | 10957 |
| 1989 | 11424 |
| 1990 | 11904 |
| 1991 | 12456 |
| 1992* | 12957 |
| 1993 | 13568 |
| 1994 | 14506 |
| 1995* | 15222 |
| 1996 | 15945 |
| 1997* | 16732 |
| 1998* | 17519 |
| 1999 | 18306 |
| 2000 | 19165 |
| 2001** | 20382 |
| 2002 | 21979 |
| 2003 | 23680 |
| 2004 | 25606 |
| 2005 | 27069 |
| 2006 | 29035 |
| 2007 | 31512 |
| 2008 | 34116 |

* Not a census year
** 2001 estimated figure from Statistics
   Canada – Source: Growth Study, 2000

Population statistics vary depending on the source. These statistics were compiled from the Government of Alberta and the City of Airdrie.

# further reading

Acme and District Historical Society. Acme Memories. Friesen Printers. Calgary, Alberta, Canada, 1979.*

Beiseker Historical Society. Beiseker's Golden Heritage. Friesen Printers. Calgary, Alberta, Canada, 1977.*

Berry, Susan and Jack Brink. Aboriginal Cultures in Alberta – Five Hundred Generations. Provincial Museum of Alberta. Published by The University of Alberta, 2007.

Byfield, Ted (Editor). Alberta in the 20th Century. Volume Two, the Birth of the Province 1900-1910. United Western Communications Ltd., 2001.

Crossfield History Committee. Prairie Sod and Goldenrod. Friesen Printers. Calgary, Alberta, Canada, 1977.*

Fleming, R. B. The Railway King of Canada. Sir William Mackenzie, 1849–1923. University of British Columbia Press. Vancouver, British Columbia, 1991.

Hicken, Sophi. Still Standing: The Grain Elevators of Southern Alberta. 1999.

Holt, Faye Reineberg. Sharing the Good Times: History of Prairie Women's Joys and Pleasures. Detselig Enterprises Ltd. Calgary, Alberta, Canada, 2000.

Holt, Faye Reineberg. Threshing: The Early Years of Harvesting. Fifth House Publishers. Calgary, Alberta, Canada, 1999.

Huck, Barbara and Doug Whiteway. In Search of Ancient Alberta: Seeking the Spirit of the Land. Published by Heartland Associates, 1998.

Klassen, Henry C. A Business History of Alberta. University of Calgary Press, 1999.

Read, Tracey. Acres and Empires: A History of the Municipal District of Rocky View no. 44. 1983.*

Wilk, Stephen. One Day's Journey. A to Zee Printing. Calgary, Alberta, Canada, 2002.*

Wilk, Stephen and Valerie Jobson & Redvers Perry. 100 Years of Nose Creek Valley History. Published by the Nose Creek Valley Historical Society. A to Zee Printing. Calgary, Alberta, Canada, 1997.*

Woolliams, Edith. My Neighbour and Yours. Friesen Printers. Calgary, Alberta, Canada, 1982.*

*Note – these books are available to view online at the "Our Roots" website listed in this section.

## Websites

Alberta Grain Elevator Society
www.grainelevators-alberta.ca

Alberta Museums Association
www.museumsalberta.ab.ca

Atlas of Alberta Railways
http://railways-atlas.tapor.ualberta.ca

City of Airdrie
www.airdrie.ca

Glenbow Museum – Collections and Research
www.glenbow.org/collections

Monklands Online – Airdrie and Monklands, Scotland
www.monklands.co.uk/airdrie/
www.monklands.co.uk/monklands/

Our Future, Our Past: Alberta Heritage Digitization Project
www.ourfutureourpast.ca

Our Roots – Canada's Local Histories Online
www.ourroots.ca

Peel's Prairie Provinces – University of Alberta Libraries
http://peel.library.ualberta.ca/index.html

Southern Alberta Pioneers and Their Descendants
http://pioneersalberta.org

The Bert Sheppard Stockmen's Foundation Library and Archives
www.smflibrary.ca/library.html

Provincial Archives of Alberta
http://hermis.cd.gov.ab.ca/paa/Default.aspx

Women of Aspenland – Images from Central Alberta
www.albertasource.ca/aspenland/eng/region/region_cities_towns.html

## Resources for young people

Alberta – How the West Was Young
www.abheritage.ca/alberta

The Canadian Encyclopedia – Youth Encyclopedia
www.thecanadianencyclopedia.com

# about the author

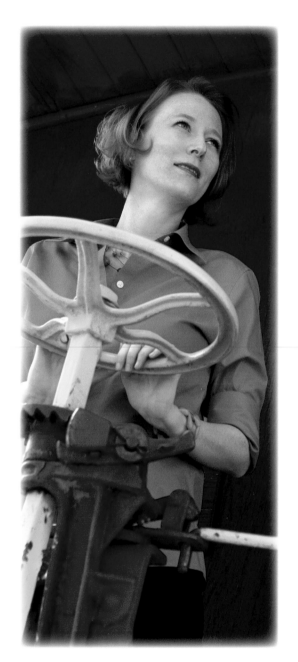

Anna Rebus received a B.A. in Geography ('96) and B.A. in Archaeology ('99) from the University of Calgary. In 2005, she received an M.A. in Museum Studies from the University of Leicester, England. In addition to her academic background, her interest in the heritage field developed through her work in Calgary at the University of Calgary, Parks Canada, the Nickle Arts Museum, Cantos Music Foundation and the Glenbow Museum. Mrs. Rebus has also spent many summers working as an archaeologist in the Four Corners region of southwest Colorado, USA. Prior to her involvement with the Airdrie Centennial project, Mrs. Rebus spent three years working for the South Australian Department for Environment and Heritage. In South Australia, she was active as the state representative for the Interpretation Australia Association and as a committee member for Museums Australia. Her publications include numerous social studies reference text and library books for elementary and junior high schools, book chapters, interpretive guides and signs, magazine and journal articles.

*end notes*

## END NOTES PART ONE: PIONEER SPIRIT

Any excerpt from *The Airdrie News* or *The Airdrie Recorder* newspapers were taken from microfilm and hard copies held at the Glenbow Archives in Calgary, Alberta.

1.  Stephen Wilk, ed. 100 Years of Nose Creek Valley History (Calgary: Nose Creek Historical Society, 1997) 50.

2.  Stephen Wilk, ed. 100 Years of Nose Creek Valley History (Calgary: Nose Creek Historical Society, 1997) 100.

3.  "History of Black Diamond," 22 April 2008
    http://www.town.blackdiamond.ab.ca/tourism/history.html

4.  Stephen Wilk, One Day's Journey (Calgary: A to Zee Printing, 2002) 246-247.

5.  Stephen Wilk, One Day's Journey (Calgary: A to Zee Printing, 2002) 246-247.

6.  Stephen Wilk, One Day's Journey (Calgary: A to Zee Printing, 2002) 39.

7.  Stephen Wilk, ed. 100 Years of Nose Creek Valley History (Calgary: Nose Creek Historical Society, 1997) 134.

8.  Stephen Wilk, One Day's Journey (Calgary: A to Zee Printing, 2002) 52.

9.  Stephen Wilk, ed. 100 Years of Nose Creek Valley History (Calgary: Nose Creek Historical Society, 1997) 64.

10. Stephen Wilk, ed. 100 Years of Nose Creek Valley History (Calgary: Nose Creek Historical Society, 1997) 64.

11. Southern Alberta Pioneers and Their Descendants – Pioneer Profiles, "Johnston Stevenson," 7 March 2006, 28 March 2008
    http://www.pioneersalberta.org/profiles/s2.html#stevenson

12. Major General T. Bland Strange, The Story of Riel's Revolt. Canada: 1885, Gaslight etexts, 17 March 2000, 28 March 2008
    http://gaslight.mtroyal.ca/revoltx2.htm

13. Archie Bushfield, John Bushfield, Cindy Carmichael, Mike Dockman and Dave Hellard (Sharp Hill Developments),
    Sharp Hill – Alberta's Only Stage Coach Robbery (booklet). A short video based on this booklet is available to view at
    http://www.casttv.com/video/lhgr9h1/attv-canadian-wild-west-episode-5-of-6-video

14. Mark Anderako, "Historic Trails – The Calgary-Edmonton Trail," book excerpt in Alberta TrailTracker – Alberta Trailnet
    Newsletter, Issue 4, December 2002:3, 14 March 2008
    http://www.albertatrailnet.com/downloads/December2002.pdf

15. Stephen Wilk, One Day's Journey (Calgary: A to Zee Printing, 2002) 275.

16. University of Alberta Press, "The Calgary and Edmonton Railway," Atlas of Alberta Railways, 2005, 11 March 2008
    http://railways-atlas.tapor.ualberta.ca/cocoon/atlas/Chapters-7-3/

17. Willis, Michael, "The Calgary and Edmonton Railway Company," Prairie Rails, 23 October 2000, 19 February 2008
    http://www.prairierails.net/calg_edm.htm

18. Stephen Wilk, One Day's Journey (Calgary: A to Zee Printing, 2002) 157.

19. Geographic Board of Canada – Department of the Interior, Place-names of Alberta, 1928, Peel's Prairie Provinces 5240, 28
    January 2008
    http://peel.library.ualberta.ca/bibliography/5240/11.html?qid=peelbib%7Cairdrie%7C%28digstatus%3Amounted%29%7Cs
    core

20.  The Airdrie Page, "The Meaning of Airdrie," Directory for Airdrie, Scotland, UK, 13 March 2008
     http://www.airdrie.net/weblog2/category/history-of-airdrie/

21.  Ian Kendall, "Scottish Place Names, Calgary, Alberta, Canada," April 2008, 25 April 2008
     http://www.rampantscotland.com/placenames/placename_calgary.htm

22.  R.B. Fleming, The Railway King of Canada – Sir William Mackenzie 1849-1923 (Vancouver: UBC Press, 1991).

23.  Library and Archives Canada, "Sir William Mackenzie," Dictionary of Canadian Biography Online, 2005, 27 February 2008.
     http://www.biographi.ca/EN/ShowBio.asp?BioId=42393

24.  P. Turner Bone, When the Steel Went Through – Reminiscences of a Railroad Pioneer (Toronto: MacMillan, 1947), 1 February 2008
     http://www.electricscotland.com/history/canada/steel15.htm

25.  Stephen Wilk, One Day's Journey (Calgary: A to Zee Printing, 2002) 157-160.

26.  Stanley Brooker, "Locations Lived In and Occupations 1908-1977," Stanley Brooker fonds at Glenbow Archives, Calgary, Alberta, Call number M 140.

27.  Stephen Wilk, One Day's Journey (Calgary: A to Zee Printing, 2002) 163-165.

28.  Government of Alberta – Municipal Affairs, "City of Airdrie Incorporation History," 14 April 2008
     http://www.municipalaffairs.gov.ab.ca/cfml/profiles/munctype_01.pdf

29.  Stephen Wilk, One Day's Journey (Calgary: A to Zee Printing, 2002) 165-166.

30.  Canadian Pacific Railway, Western Lines, Industrial Department, Manufacturing and Business Opportunities in Western Canada Along the Lines of the Canadian Pacific Railway (Winnipeg: Industrial Department, Western Lines, 1910), Peel's Prairie Provinces 3393, 28 January 2008
     http://peel.library.ualberta.ca/bibliography/3393/116.html?qid=peelbib%7Cairdrie%7C%28digstatus%3Amounted%29%7Cscore

31.  Stephen Wilk, One Day's Journey (Calgary: A to Zee Printing, 2002) 160-161.

32.  Flett's Blacksmith Shop and Airdrie House, archives provided by Heritage Park Historical Village, Calgary, Alberta, March 2008.

33.  The City of Red Deer, "Red Deer Centre Women's Institute Constituency Fonds MG 173," March 2008, 24 April 2008
     http://www.reddeer.ca/NR/rdonlyres/B729F345-D739-43BC-A98D-E82F566B3B95/0/FindingAidofRedDeerCentreWomensConsituencyWI.pdf

34.  Stephen Wilk, One Day's Journey (Calgary: A to Zee Printing, 2002) 346-349.

35.  Stephen Wilk, ed. 100 Years of Nose Creek Valley History (Calgary: Nose Creek Historical Society, 1997) 137.

36.  Violet Hatt-Bailey, Airdrie – The Way I Remember (Personal family history booklet printed ca. 1990s).

37.  Stephen Wilk, One Day's Journey (Calgary: A to Zee Printing, 2002) 299.

38.  Stephen Wilk, One Day's Journey (Calgary: A to Zee Printing, 2002) 362.

39.  Canadian Fallen Heroes Foundation, Memorial Prints on display at the Nose Creek Valley Museum, Airdrie, Alberta, 2008.

40.  Stephen Wilk, One Day's Journey (Calgary: A to Zee Printing, 2002) 166-167.

41. Stanley Brooker, "Locations Lived In and Occupations 1908-1977," Stanley Brooker fonds at Glenbow Archives, Calgary, Alberta, Call number M 140.

42. Ted Byfield, et al., The Great War and Its Consequences 1914-1920, Alberta in the 20th Century Volume 4 (Edmonton, AB: United Western Communications Ltd, 1995) 5.

43. Stephen Wilk, One Day's Journey (Calgary: A to Zee Printing, 2002) 176-180.

44. Archives Society of Alberta, "Alberta Wheat Pool," ASA Newsletter, Volume 22, Number 1, Fall 2002, 5 May 2008 http://www.archivesalberta.org/vol22_1/glenbow.htm

45. Stephen Wilk, One Day's Journey (Calgary: A to Zee Printing, 2002) 204.

46. Stephen Wilk, One Day's Journey (Calgary: A to Zee Printing, 2002) 204.

47. Stephen Wilk, One Day's Journey (Calgary: A to Zee Printing, 2002) 206.

48. Alberta Electric System Operator, Powering Albertans Newsletter, Spring 2008:5.

49. Transalta Utilities Corporation, "2006 Renewal Annual Information Form for the Year Ended December 31, 2005," 22 March 2006, 3 May 2008 http://www.transalta.com/transalta/webcms.nsf/AllDoc/DB2DD20DF09203AC872571AE0079BBD7/$File/2006%20TAU%20 AIF%20Final.pdf

50. Stephen Wilk, One Day's Journey (Calgary: A to Zee Printing, 2002) 310-313.

51. Stephen Wilk, One Day's Journey (Calgary: A to Zee Printing, 2002) 162.

52. Stephen Wilk, One Day's Journey (Calgary: A to Zee Printing, 2002) 198.

53. Airdrie Mutual Telephone Company fonds at Glenbow Archives, Calgary, Alberta, Call number M 2247.

54. Stephen Wilk, One Day's Journey (Calgary: A to Zee Printing, 2002) 199.

55. Chester Fowler and Margaret Fowler, personal interview, 6 December 2007.

56. Jim Hole and Joann Jones-Hole, personal interview, 23 November 2007.

57. Calgary Bull Sale, Ranching Community Showcase, 4 March 2006, 21 April 2008. http://www.calgarybullsale.com/news-040306.htm

58. Brendan Wood, "Hanson Family Lives the Western Tradition," Airdrie Echo 27 July 2005, 20 March 2008 http://cgi.bowesonline.com/pedro.php?id=63&x=story&xid=174992

59. James (Jim) and Jessie Bussey, personal interview, 6 December 2007.

60. Canadian Wheat Board Annual Report 2005-2006, 17 March 2008 http://www.cwb.ca/public/en/about/investor/annual/pdf/05-06/2005-06_annual-report.pdf

61. Stephen Wilk, One Day's Journey (Calgary: A to Zee Printing, 2002) 256-257.

62. Canadian Fallen Heroes Foundation, Memorial Prints on display at the Nose Creek Valley Museum, Airdrie, Alberta, 2008.

63. "World War II and POW Camps in Canada," Alberta Online Encyclopedia 2002, 24 January 2008 http://www.albertasource.ca/lawcases/criminal/powmurder/setting_camps_canada.htm

64. Glenbow Archives, Calgary, Alberta, Photo archive NA-4159-23, 29 January 2008, http://ww2.glenbow.org/search/archivesPhotosSearch.aspx

65. Lilly Jensen, personal interview, 6 February 2008.

66. ATCO Group, "History, 1950s," 13 March 2008 http://www.atco.com/About+Us/History/Share+Our+Journey+1950s.htm

67. Stephen Wilk, One Day's Journey (Calgary: A to Zee Printing, 2002) 248.

68. Stephen Wilk, One Day's Journey (Calgary: A to Zee Printing, 2002) 250-252.

69. Glenbow Archives, Calgary, Alberta, Photo archive NA-5600-7208a and NA-5600-7208b, 29 January 2008, http://ww2.glenbow.org/search/archivesPhotosSearch.aspx.

70. Stephen Wilk, ed. 100 Years of Nose Creek Valley History (Calgary: Nose Creek Historical Society, 1997) 205-206.

71. Alberta Municipal Affairs, City of Airdrie – Population Statistics 1913 -1971.

72. Stephen Wilk, ed. 100 Years of Nose Creek Valley History (Calgary: Nose Creek Historical Society, 1997) 208.

73. George McDougall High School, "Course Information Handbook 2008-2009," 5 May 2008 http://www.rockyview.ab.ca/mcdougall/frames/main/GMHS%20Course%20Handbook%2008-09.pdf

74. Industry Canada, "Canadian Company Capabilities," 7 May 2008 http://strategis.ic.gc.ca/app/ccc/srch/nvgt.do?lang=eng&app=1&prtl=1&sbPrtl=&estblmntNo=123456087421&profile=cmpltPrfl

75. Stephen Wilk, ed. 100 Years of Nose Creek Valley History (Calgary: Nose Creek Historical Society, 1997) 207.

76. Stephen Wilk, ed. 100 Years of Nose Creek Valley History (Calgary: Nose Creek Historical Society, 1997) 208.

77. Stephen Wilk, ed. 100 Years of Nose Creek Valley History (Calgary: Nose Creek Historical Society, 1997) 217.

78. Stephen Wilk, ed. 100 Years of Nose Creek Valley History (Calgary: Nose Creek Historical Society, 1997) 216.

79. Government of Alberta – Municipal Affairs, "City of Airdrie Incorporation History," 14 April 2008 http://www.municipalaffairs.gov.ab.ca/cfml/profiles/munctype_01.pdf

80. Stephen Wilk, ed. 100 Years of Nose Creek Valley History (Calgary: Nose Creek Historical Society, 1997) 208.

81. Stephen Wilk, ed. 100 Years of Nose Creek Valley History (Calgary: Nose Creek Historical Society, 1997) 216.

82. Stephen Wilk, ed. 100 Years of Nose Creek Valley History (Calgary: Nose Creek Historical Society, 1997) 218.

83. Rol-land Farms Ltd., 30 April 2008 http://rollandfarms.com/index.html

84. BURNCO Rock Products Ltd., "The Third Generation," 27 April 2008 http://www.burnco.com/RetailWeb/web/corporate/gen3.aspx

85. Propak Systems Ltd., 24 April 2008 http://www.propaksystems.com/

86. Old Dutch Snack Foods Ltd., "Chronological Timeline," 18 May 2008 http://olddutchfoods.ca/eng/chronological_timeline.html

87. Brooke Hogemann, "City boasts vibrant industrial sector," <u>Airdrie Echo</u> 18 August 2004, 7 May 2008
http://cgi.bowesonline.com/pedro.php?id=63&x=story&xid=113404

88. Government of Alberta – Municipal Affairs, "City of Airdrie Incorporation History," 14 April 2008
http://www.municipalaffairs.gov.ab.ca/cfml/profiles/munctype_01.pdf

89. "Airdrie Year in Review," <u>Airdrie Echo</u> 28 December 2005, 15 April 2008
http://cgi.bowesonline.com/pedro.php?id=63&x=story&xid=204323

90. Anne Beaty and Scott Mitchell, "Future begins to take shape in city's downtown," <u>Airdrie Echo</u> 26 March 2008, 26 April 2008
http://cgi.bowesonline.com/pedro.php?id=63&x=story&xid=387348

91. Heloise Lorimer, personal interview, 6 February 2008.

92. Mike Ploner, "Five die in CP train crash," <u>Airdrie and District Echo</u> 30 March 1983:1.

93. Stephen Wilk, ed. <u>100 Years of Nose Creek Valley History</u> (Calgary: Nose Creek Historical Society, 1997) 212.

94. Janice Iverson, "Stranded strangers wait out blizzard in city," Airdrie Echo 21 May 1986:1.

95. Ian Tennant, "Oh baby, what a storm," Airdrie Echo 21 May 1986:1.

96. Stephen Wilk, ed. 100 Years of Nose Creek Valley History (Calgary: Nose Creek Historical Society, 1997) 15-18.

97. "Torch ceremony does city proud," <u>Airdrie Echo</u> 17 February 1988:3.

98. Greg Gatin, "Airdrie business celebrates 50th," <u>Airdrie Echo</u> 13 July 1994.

99. Anne Beaty, "Nose Creek officially opens," <u>Airdrie Echo</u> 14 September 1994:9.

100. Lilly Jensen, personal interview, 6 February 2008.

101. Airdrie Festival of Lights, 20 December 2008
http://www.airdriefestivaloflights.com/

102. Information on twinning with Airdrie, Scotland provided by Mary Hickley, personal notes, March 2008.

103. Information on twinning with Yuto-Cho, Japan provided by the City of Airdrie, April 2008.

104. Information on twinning with Gwacheon City, South Korea provided by the City of Airdrie, April 2008.

105. City of Airdrie, "Population growth," 16 January 2009.
http://www.airdrie.ca/economic_development/business_attraction/population_growth.cfm

106. Michael J. Knell, "Palliser will close Alberta leather factory, shift work," <u>Furniture Today</u> 2 July 2007, 7 May 2008
http://www.furnituretoday.com/article/CA6457332.html?display=News

107. "Local swimmer achieves dream," <u>Airdrie Echo</u> 9 April 2008, 8 May 2008.
http://cgi.bowesonline.com/pedro.php?id=63&x=story&xid=391434

108. Scott Mitchell, "Airdrie BMX," <u>Airdrie Echo</u> 16 April 2008, 8 May 2008
http://cgi.bowesonline.com/pedro.php?id=63&x=story&xid=392996

109. Kraft Hockeyville, 18 December 2008,
http://www.cbc.ca/sports/hockey/hockeyville/

110. "AirdrieLIFE is...Hockeyville!" <u>AirdrieLIFE</u>, Volume 1, Fall/Winter 2006:13-18,
http://www.airdrielife.com/pdf/AirdrieLIFE_fall2006.pdf

## END NOTES PART TWO: COMMUNITY PRIDE

Any excerpt from *The Airdrie News* or *The Airdrie Recorder* newspapers were taken from microfilm and hard copies held at the Glenbow Archives in Calgary, Alberta.

1.  All information on Dr. Edwards from: Jean M. Edwards, Our Family History (Personal family history booklet printed ca. early 2000s).

2.  Letter from the archives at Nose Creek Valley Museum.

3.  Heloise Lorimer, personal interview, 6 February 2008.

4.  Marilyn McCall, personal interview, 29 November 2007.

5.  Brian Jackson, personal interview and correspondence, 6 May 2008.

6.  Paul Brandt website, 2 January 2009
    http://www.paulbrandt.com

7.  Linda Bruce, personal interview, 3 December 2007.

8.  Tim Harriman, personal interview, 13 February 2008.

9.  Information on Robin Burwash from personal correspondence, 24 June 2008.

10. Doug Nelson, Hotcakes to High Stakes: The Chuckwagon Story (Detselig Enterprises Ltd. 1993) 138.

11. Additional information about Ron David submitted by Kathy Lind (mother of Jim Nevada) 26 March 2008

12. World Professional Chuckwagon Association, Chad Fike Biography, 17 January 2009
    http://www.wpca.com/(S(agkiy0yeodzq3o45r5ndhha0))/profile_detail.aspx?ID=65

13. Canadian Professional Rodeo Hall of Fame, 2002 Hall of Fame inductee Jim Dunn, 16 January 2009
    http://www.canadianprorodeohalloffame.com/inductees.php?year=2002

14. Canadian Professional Rodeo Hall of Fame, 2002 Hall of Fame inductee Jim Dunn, 16 January 2009
    http://www.canadianprorodeohalloffame.com/inductees.php?year=2002

15. Canadian Cowboy Country Magazine December/January 2005
    Jim Dunn 2004 Canadian Professional Rodeo Association Cowboy of the Year
    http://www.canadiancowboy.ca/inthecorral/dec-jan05.html

16. Information on Jim Nevada submitted by Kathy Lind (mother of Jim Nevada) 26 March 2008. See also: Glen Mikkelsen, Never Holler Whoa! The Cowboys of Chuckwagon Racing (Balmur Book Publishing, 2000).

17. Atlas Lumber Yard history provided by Heritage Park Historical Village, Calgary, Alberta, 13 March 2008.

18. Dates for the exact opening of The Old Hotel vary depending on the source. Page 247 of One Day's Journey by Stephen Wilk indicates that Dan McDonald (also spelled MacDonald) started up the hotel in 1904. Page 157 of One Day's Journey by Stephen Wilk indicates that "In 1902, R.A. McDonald moved a dwelling from the Bert Carlson farm, next to the Croxford home and started a boarding house." Page 67 of 100 Years of Nose Creek Valley History by Stephen Wilk identifies The Old Hotel as having been a stopping point for travelers since 1912. Page 206 of 100 Years of Nose Creek Valley History by Stephen Wilk mentions that old photographs indicate the hotel was there by 1907.

19.  Stephen Wilk, One Day's Journey (Calgary: A to Zee Printing, 2002) 129.

20.  "Prohibition," Alberta Online Encyclopedia – The Famous 5, Heroes for Today, 12 January 2009
     http://www.abheritage.ca/famous5/achievements/prohibition.html

21.  "Alberta Liquor Plebiscite 1957," Wikipedia, 20 December 2008
     http://en.wikipedia.org/wiki/1957_Alberta_Liquor_Plebiscite
     The ban on mixed drinking was lifted in Calgary, Edmonton, Gleichen, Banff – Cochrane and Cloverbar in 1957.

22.  "A Short History of Liquor Regulations in Alberta," Alberta Liquor and Gaming Commission, 9 January 2009
     http://www.aglc.gov.ab.ca/liquor/historyofliquorregulations.asp
     The ban on mixed drinking was lifted in the rest of Alberta in 1967.

23.  Ada Ryan written account, 11 November 1962. Stephen Wilk Airdrie History collection, Glenbow Archives, Calgary, Alberta.

24.  Stephen Wilk, ed. 100 Years of Nose Creek Valley History (Calgary: Nose Creek Historical Society, 1997) 118.

25.  The Alberta-Pacific Elevator Company was founded in 1907. The September 8, 1909 edition of The Airdrie News indicates the construction of the Alberta-Pacific grain elevator in Airdrie was nearing completion. In 1912 the company merged with the Alberta Grain Company to form the Alberta Pacific Grain Company. Glenbow Archives, Calgary, Alberta – Alberta-Pacific Grain Company fonds.

26.  Stephen Wilk, One Day's Journey (Calgary: A to Zee Printing, 2002) 262.

27.  Stephen Wilk, One Day's Journey (Calgary: A to Zee Printing, 2002) 261.

28.  The Jack Dawson story was provided by the Nose Creek Valley Museum.

29.  William Evans interview transcripts, 1962. Stephen Wilk Airdrie History collection – Glenbow Archives, Calgary, Alberta.

30.  Stephen Wilk, One Day's Journey (Calgary: A to Zee Printing, 2002) 193.

31.  Stories and reminiscences about Airdrie United Church suppers were gathered from numerous longtime Airdrie residents.

32.  Stories and reminiscences about the Handy Lunch (Jock's) were gathered from numerous longtime Airdrie residents.

33.  Stephen Wilk, One Day's Journey (Calgary: A to Zee Printing, 2002) 167.

34.  Airdrie Airport write-up submitted by Trevor McTavish (edited for word count).

35.  Information on the Jolly Shopper was gathered from Johnnie Loveday's daughter, Janet (Loveday) Mason and numerous longtime Airdrie residents.

36.  Dusan's Clothing Store write-up submitted by Tom Milutinovic and members of the Milutinovic family.

37.  Stephen Wilk, ed. 100 Years of Nose Creek Valley History (Calgary: Nose Creek Historical Society, 1997) 208.

38.  Karen Lazaruk, "Water Tower Saved – Council Unanimously Opposes Recommendation to Dismantle Airdrie Landmark and Sell Lot," Airdrie Echo 20 August 2003, 19 November 2008
     http://cgi.bowesonline.com/pedro.php?id=63&x=story&xid=71434

39.  Airdrie Public Library write-up submitted by the Airdrie Public Library (edited for word count).

40.  Information on the Environmental Education Centre provided by the City of Airdrie.

41. Anne Beaty, "Canadian Municipalities Learn About 'Green' Living From Airdrie, Alberta," Airdrie Echo 8 August 2007, 6 January 2009
http://cgi.bowesonline.com/pedro.php?id=63&x=story&xid=329195

42. Bylaws and council meeting minutes available at The Alberta Heritage Digitization Project – Municipal Bylaws of Alberta
http://www.ourfutureourpast.ca

43. Stephen Wilk, ed. 100 Years of Nose Creek Valley History (Calgary: Nose Creek Historical Society, 1997) 207.

44. Stephen Wilk, ed. 100 Years of Nose Creek Valley History (Calgary: Nose Creek Historical Society, 1997) 207.

45. Stephen Wilk, ed. 100 Years of Nose Creek Valley History (Calgary: Nose Creek Historical Society, 1997) 207.

46. Staffing figures provided by the City of Airdrie.

47. Stephen Wilk, One Day's Journey (Calgary: A to Zee Printing, 2002) 157.

48. "Arthur E. Bowers History," A.E. Bowers Elementary School, 10 January 2009
http://plone.rockyview.ab.ca/bowers/school-info/a-e-bowers-history/?searchterm=history

49. Stephen Wilk, One Day's Journey (Calgary: A to Zee Printing, 2002) 327.

50. Anne Beaty, "Bronze Art Graces City," Airdrie Echo 12 September 2007, 17 April 2008
http://cgi.bowesonline.com/pedro.php?id=63&x=story&xid=337888

51. Myke Thomas, "Reunion Keeps Hopewell Traditions Alive," Calgary Sun 1 September 2007, 17 April 2008
http://www.calgarysun.com/cgi-bin/publish.cgi?p=195535&s=homes&x=articles

52. Cooper's Crossing, "The First Family to Move Here Stayed 100 Years," 20 November 2008
http://www.cooperscrossing.ca/history.html

53. Stephen Wilk, One Day's Journey (Calgary: A to Zee Printing, 2002) 157.

54. Stephen Wilk, One Day's Journey (Calgary: A to Zee Printing, 2002) 248.

55. Stephen Wilk, One Day's Journey (Calgary: A to Zee Printing, 2002) 168.

56. Stephen Wilk, ed. 100 Years of Nose Creek Valley History (Calgary: Nose Creek Historical Society, 1997) 207.

57. Stephen Wilk, One Day's Journey (Calgary: A to Zee Printing, 2002) 198.

58. Stephen Wilk, One Day's Journey (Calgary: A to Zee Printing, 2002) 166.

59. Stephen Wilk, One Day's Journey (Calgary: A to Zee Printing, 2002) 166.

60. Heritage Park Historical Village, Calgary, Alberta.

61. Calgary Stampede Rangeland Derby "Past Champions,"
http://old.cs.calgarystampede.com/chuckwagons/chucks/rangeland_derby/past_champions.html

62. Stephen Wilk, ed. 100 Years of Nose Creek Valley History (Calgary: Nose Creek Historical Society, 1997) 149.

63. Stephen Wilk, One Day's Journey (Calgary: A to Zee Printing, 2002) 120.

64. Stephen Wilk, ed. 100 Years of Nose Creek Valley History (Calgary: Nose Creek Historical Society, 1997) 209.

65. "Hawkeys have rich heritage in Alberta," Airdrie Echo 27 June 1984:28.

66. Stephen Wilk, ed. 100 Years of Nose Creek Valley History (Calgary: Nose Creek Historical Society, 1997) 173.

67. Stephen Wilk, One Day's Journey (Calgary: A to Zee Printing, 2002) 178.

68. "Our School's History," R.J. Hawkey Elementary School, 14 January 2009
    http://plone.rockyview.ab.ca/rjhawkey/our-school/r-j-hawkey-elementary-schools-history/

69. Stephen Wilk, One Day's Journey (Calgary: A to Zee Printing, 2002) 243.

70. Stephen Wilk, One Day's Journey (Calgary: A to Zee Printing, 2002) 244.

71. Iron Horse Park, Miniature Railway, 16 January 2009
    http://www.ironhorsepark.net

72. Lilly Jensen, personal interview, 6 February 2008.

73. Stephen Wilk, One Day's Journey (Calgary: A to Zee Printing, 2002) 99.

74. Stephen Wilk, One Day's Journey (Calgary: A to Zee Printing, 2002) 165.

75. Stephen Wilk, ed. 100 Years of Nose Creek Valley History (Calgary: Nose Creek Historical Society, 1997) 207.

76. Elaine McCracken, personal interview, 3 December 2007.

77. Personal communication – Elaine McKee-Doel, 17 March 2008

78. "Building a Legacy – City Honours Airdrie Builder," AirdrieLIFE. Volume 4, Number 1, Fall 2007:48.
    http://www.airdrielife.com/pdf/AirdrieLIFE_fall2007.pdf

79. Monklands Online, "Monklands: Ancient Condition of the Parish in 1160 – Brief History of the Area," 10 January 2009
    http://www.monklands.co.uk/monklands/

80. Stephen Wilk, One Day's Journey (Calgary: A to Zee Printing, 2002) 253.

81. Stephen Wilk, ed. 100 Years of Nose Creek Valley History (Calgary: Nose Creek Historical Society, 1997) 207.

82. Stephen Wilk, ed. 100 Years of Nose Creek Valley History (Calgary: Nose Creek Historical Society, 1997) 213.

83. Stephen Wilk, ed. 100 Years of Nose Creek Valley History (Calgary: Nose Creek Historical Society, 1997) 213.

84. "Muriel Clayton's History," Muriel Clayton Middle School, 10 January 2009 (all information from this website)
    http://plone.rockyview.ab.ca/mclayton/our-school

85. Marilyn McCall, personal interview, 29 November 2007.

86. Information about Ted Lord taken from the plaque at Ted Lord Memorial Park, Airdrie, Alberta.

87. Stephen Wilk, One Day's Journey (Calgary: A to Zee Printing, 2002) 244.

88. Stephen Wilk, One Day's Journey (Calgary: A to Zee Printing, 2002) 298.

89. Stephen Wilk, One Day's Journey (Calgary: A to Zee Printing, 2002) 242.

90. Stephen Wilk, One Day's Journey (Calgary: A to Zee Printing, 2002) 244.

91. Stephen Wilk, One Day's Journey (Calgary: A to Zee Printing, 2002) 167.

92. National Defence, "Year of the Veteran: Canada Pays Tribute," Canadian Forces Personnel Newsletter, Issue 1/05 – 26 January 2005, 16 January 2009
http://www.forces.gc.ca/hr/cfpn/engraph/1_05/1_05_yov_e.asp

93. Brendan Wood, "Airdrie's Roads Honour War Veterans, Settlers," Airdrie Echo 17 August 2005, 20 December 2008
http://cgi.bowesonline.com/pedro.php?id=63&x=story&xid=178878

94. R.B. Fleming, The Railway King of Canada – Sir William Mackenzie 1849-1923 (Vancouver: UBC Press, 1991).

95. Stephen Wilk, One Day's Journey (Calgary: A to Zee Printing, 2002) 115.

96. Local clubs, organizations and societies submitted information and write-ups for inclusion within this section. Write-ups were edited for style and word count. Information was also gathered from club websites when available.

97. "New Year, New Record," Airdrie City View 9 January 2009, 17 January 2009
http://www.airdriecityview.com/pdf_pages/Jan8/Page06.pdf

98. Stephen Wilk, One Day's Journey (Calgary: A to Zee Printing, 2002) 337.

99. Stephen Wilk, One Day's Journey (Calgary: A to Zee Printing, 2002) 339.

**END NOTES PART THREE: OPPORTUNITY FOR THE FUTURE**

1. Information on The Natural Step Program provided by the City of Airdrie. See also
http://www.thenaturalstep.org/en/canada/

2. Information on downtown redevelopment provided by the City of Airdrie, 15 April 2008. See also
http://www.airdrie.ca/building_development/planning/city_plans.cfm

*photo credits*

## PHOTO CREDITS

Every effort has been made to give credit for use of images. It has been challenging effort in that many historic photos have been shared, passed around between family and friends, and copied. We have credited the source that the Airdrie Centennial Committee received its images from – this may or may not be the original owner or photographer. Any oversights or omissions is regrettable.

### Page IX
Airdrie Centennial History Committee – Larry Bilben

### Page XIII
Passengers (including Reeve Knud Jensen) enjoying a trip on a replica stagecoach as they celebrate historic travel along the Calgary to Edmonton Trail 1955 – Janet (Loveday) Mason

### Page XX
Airdrie ca. 1910, photo by Dr. W.F. Edwards – Jean M. Edwards, Our Family History
(Personal family history booklet printed ca. early 2000s)

### Page XXI
Aerial view of Airdrie 2008 – City of Airdrie

### Page XXIII
Suburban Airdrie – City of Airdrie


## PHOTO CREDITS PART ONE: PIONEER SPIRIT

### Page 25
(Pioneer spirit)
Plowing the land – Heloise Lorimer (All photos courtesy of Heloise Lorimer come from the Van Sickle family album)

### Page 26
Woman in front of house – Thomas Howe; Children – Heloise Lorimer

### Page 27
(Early pioneer spirit)
Dragging on the land for spring wheat – Heloise Lorimer

### Page 28
Stagecoach – Janet (Loveday) Mason; Wheel – Anna Rebus

### Page 29
Major General T. Bland Strange – Glenbow Archives NA 1847-2

**Page 30**
Stagecoach – Glenbow Archives NA 1162-3

**Page 31**
Stagecoach – Glenbow Archives NA 1905-1; Dickson-Stevenson Stopping House – Glenbow Archives NA 582-1; Addison D. McPherson – Glenbow Archives NA 2354-6

**Page 32**
Railway scene – Glenbow Archives NA 1231-1; Locomotive – Heloise Lorimer

**Page 33**
Railway track and wheel – Anna Rebus; Sir William Mackenzie – National Archives of Canada/Image in public domain; Airdrie station – Heloise Lorimer

**Page 34**
Sod turning ceremony – Glenbow Archives NA 3320-8

**Page 35**
Workers playing poker – Glenbow Archives NA 1905-13; Railway construction work – Glenbow Archives NA 1905-15

**Page 36**
Airdrie street scene – Heloise Lorimer; House – Heloise Lorimer

**Page 37**
Van Sickle family home – Heloise Lorimer; Land advertisement – Glenbow Archives NA 3765-4; Croxford family home – Nose Creek Valley Museum

**Page 38**
(Horses, haybales and harvests)
All photos – Heloise Lorimer. Girls beside oat-stack identified in Van Sickle family album as: Edna, Nancy, and Effie May taking a sun bath beside an oat-stack.

**Page 39**
Threshing machine and farmers (1904) – Heloise Lorimer; Stanley Brooker – Glenbow Archives NA 479-28

**Page 40**
Aerial view of Airdrie – photo by Dr. W.F. Edwards; Street scene – Glenbow Archives PA 3689-335

**Page 41**
Street scene – Glenbow Archives NA 1793-1; Airdrie Hardware Co. – Nose Creek Valley Museum; Scale at Nose Creek Valley Museum – Anna Rebus

**Page 42**
Flett's Blacksmith Shop – Glenbow Archives NA 2466-1; Anvil at Nose Creek Valley Museum – Anna Rebus

**Page 43**
Flett's Blacksmith Shop – Heritage Park Historical Village, Calgary; Blacksmith tools at Heritage Park Historical Village, Calgary – Anna Rebus; W. and D. MacKay Blacksmith Shop – Glenbow Archives NA 2666-1

**Page 44**
Clothing at Nose Creek Valley Museum – Anna Rebus; Women with quilt – Lilly Jensen; Family in garden identified in Van Sickle family album as: 1913 Mother (Mrs. Van Sickle) in her garden with Heloise, Muriel, Aileen and Calvin – Heloise Lorimer

**Page 45**
Women with baby – Heloise Lorimer; Woman on horseback – Heloise Lorimer

Page 46
Bride – Margie Reid; Cow in field – Heloise Lorimer; Milk container and washboard at Nose Creek Valley Museum – Anna Rebus; Woman feeding chickens – Heloise Lorimer

**Page 47**
Threshing crew – Heloise Lorimer; Postage stamp – Nose Creek Valley Museum; Mary Morrow at Post Office – Heloise Lorimer

**Page 48**
Background image and rolling pin from Nose Creek Valley Museum – Anna Rebus; Recipe book – Elaine McCracken, Elaine McCracken – Elaine McCracken

**Page 49**
Recipe book – Elaine McCracken, Kitchen gadgets from Nose Creek Valley Museum – Anna Rebus

**Page 50**
Airdrie's first school – Nose Creek Valley Museum; School desks from Nose Creek Valley Museum – Anna Rebus

**Page 51**
Girls on horseback identified in Van Sickle family album as: 1929 (L to R) Sheila MacKay, Beryl Pike and Jessie Andrew – Heloise Lorimer; School students – Heloise Lorimer; School bell at Nose Creek Valley Museum – Sharon Bilben

**Page 52**
WWI poster by Robert Baden-Powell 1915 – image in the public domain.

**Page 53**
Influenza poster – Glenbow Archives NA 4548-5; Stanley Brooker – Glenbow Archives 479-10; Doctor's bag and implements – Anna Rebus

**Page 54**
Building barn and street scene – Heloise Lorimer

**Page 55**
Jackson Construction Company mule team – Glenbow Archives NA 2579-11; Family in front of car 1927 – Heloise Lorimer; Car auction early 1930s; Working on irrigation ditch – Heloise Lorimer

**Page 56**
Burning candle – Anna Rebus; Orvilla Kininmonth – A.J. Pearson

**Page 57**
Modern All-Electric Kitchen – Glenbow Archives NA 1846-28; Truck advertising benefits of electricity – Glenbow Archives NA 4477-48

**Page 58**
Children in front of house – Lilly Jensen; Buzz Lorimer "bat boy" 1946 – Heloise Lorimer; Group of Danish Canadians having a picnic – Lilly Jensen

**Page 59**
Group at the dinner table – Lilly Jensen; Dance at Crossfield – Nose Creek Valley Museum

**Page 60**
Aileen Van Sickle picking cucumbers – Heloise Lorimer; Man on train – Glenbow Archives NC 6-12955b

**Page 61**
Men near railway track – Glenbow Archives NC 6-12955i; Cracked soil – Anna Rebus; Pile of potatoes – Heloise Lorimer

**Page 62**
Street scene – Heloise Lorimer

**Page 63**
Telephone switchboard at Nose Creek Valley Museum – Anna Rebus; Telephone at Nose Creek Valley Museum – Sharon Bilben; Helen Moore Stewart – Roberta Whittaker; Ethel Weir – Patti (Young) Norton

**Page 64**
Arthur Hole on horseback 1950 – Glenbow Archives NA 4159-26

**Page 65**
Cliff Tebb on horseback – Olive Tebb; Jim and Jessie Bussey – Anna Rebus; Chester Fowler – Pat Jeffray; Jim Hole – Anna Rebus

**Page 66**
Postcard from World War Two – Heloise Lorimer; Orma and Bert Clayton – Heloise Lorimer

**Page 67**
War medal – Elaine McCracken; William Hegy – Bill Hegy (nephew of William)

**Page 68**
War medal – Elaine McCracken; Immigration card – Vivienne Weir; Ian and Vivienne Weir wedding photo – Sharon (Weir) Jensen; Soldier's service book – Nose Creek Valley Museum

**Page 69**
Binders at Dougan farm – Thomas Howe; War medal – Elaine McCracken; POW working on Langdon farm – Glenbow Archives NA 4519-23

**Page 70**
Gentlemen in front of car – Lilly Jensen; The Jensens and their new TV – Lilly Jensen

**Page 71**
Agricultural field days at Victor Watson's farm – Glenbow Archives NA 5600-7208b and NA 5600-6838a

**Page 72**
Children in July 1 parade 1970 – Elaine McCracken; Cowboy bull riding – Nathan Anderson

**Page 73**
Suburban Airdrie – City of Airdrie

**Page 74**
Yellow truck – Ken Morris Jr.; Water tower – Heloise Lorimer; Water tower under construction – Nose Creek Valley Museum

**Page 75**
Fire truck in garage – Elaine McCracken; Red fire truck – Marilyn McCall

**Page 76**
Dirt road to village dump – Marilyn McCall; Grain elevators – Marilyn McCall

**Page 77**
Village council members – Elaine McCracken; ATCO at Airdrie Airport – Glenbow Archives NA 5713-15

**Page 78**
Kids in parade – Nancy Jeffray; Shirley McCracken and Bonnie Clark on bikes – Elaine McCracken

**Page 79**
All photos – Nancy Jeffray

**Page 80**
Pedestrian overpass – Sharon Bilben; Darrell Bennett – City of Airdrie

**Page 81**
Airdrie Community Hall – Marilyn McCall; Town and Country Centre – Heloise Lorimer;
Airdrie's main street 1974 – Provincial Archives of Alberta GR1989.0516/0036

**Page 82**
ATCO construction site of Town of Airdrie office building – Marilyn McCall; Palliser Furniture – City of Airdrie; Money's Mushrooms – Judy Jefferies

**Page 83**
Propak Systems Ltd – Propak Systems Ltd.; Airdrie's east side 1978 – Heloise Lorimer

**Page 84**
Town of Airdrie float – Sharon Bilben; Ron Davidson – Ken Rozniak

**Page 85**

Condillo Foods – City of Airdrie; Airdrie Emergency Services – Airdrie Emergency Services; Bethany Care Centre – Bethany Care Centre

**Page 86**

Fort Towerlane – Ken Rozniak; Cutting the ribbon – Ken Rozniak; Towerlane Mall empty field – Marilyn McCall

**Page 87**

Aerial view of Airdrie – City of Airdrie

**Page 88**

Steam train – Heloise Lorimer; Railcar wheels at Nose Creek Valley Museum – Anna Rebus

**Page 89**

Steam train – Heloise Lorimer; Railcar at Nose Creek Valley Museum – Anna Rebus

**Page 90**

Jonathan and Juli Neufeld playing in snow bank – Glenda Neufeld; Backyard pictures – Marilyn McCall

**Page 91**

Cutting the ribbon – Nose Creek Valley Museum; Nose Creek Valley Museum – City of Airdrie

**Page 92**

Olympic Torch – Loreen Hamilton; Kimberly and Kari Dahl (back row) and Julianne and Jonathan Neufeld holding their Olympic "torch" candles – Glenda Neufeld

**Page 93**

Hanging the Olympic flag – Marilyn McCall; Charlotte Baumann – Ruth Baumann; Clint Bilben with Olympic mascots Heidi and Howdy – Sharon Bilben

**Page 94**

Nose Creek Park – City of Airdrie; Moving the Jensen Barn – Anthony Connolly for the *Airdrie Echo*

**Page 95**

Airdrie Festival of Lights – Airdrie Festival of Lights

**Page 96**

Dancer in front of totem – City of Airdrie

**Page 97**

Airdrie tartan – Sharon Bilben

**Page 98**

All photos – Sharon and Larry Bilben

**Page 99**

Dan Oneil in South Korea – Ed Eggerer; Airdrie Park in South Korea – Ed Eggerer

**Page 100**
The Old Hotel and lamppost – Anna Rebus

**Page 101**
Linda Bruce – City of Airdrie; 1911 Cadillac – City of Airdrie

**Page 102**
Prairie Pond Posse in convertible – AirdrieLIFE Magazine


**PHOTO CREDITS PART TWO: COMMUNITY PRIDE**

**Page 105**
(Community pride)
Airdrie baseball team, 1957 – Heloise Lorimer

**Page 107**
Three men standing on head identified in Van Sickle family album as: Frank, Fred and I (Lafe Van Sickle) doing a trick the Trinity (Ontario) boys can't do – Heloise Lorimer

**Page 108**
Jonathon Dockman, Canada Cancer Crusade – City of Airdrie; Oyster supper 1955 – Heloise Lorimer; RCMP in July 1 Parade – City of Airdrie; Working in the flower beds – City of Airdrie

**Page 109**
Airdrie and District Rotary Club Soap Box Derby – City of Airdrie; Airdrie Show and Shine at Nose Creek Park – City of Airdrie; Alan Tennant with shaved head raising funds for Hospice Calgary 1998 – Alan Tennant; Miss Leanne Percy, Miss Rodeo Airdrie 2005 – City of Airdrie; Ken Reid, Marge Uhrich and Frank Reid ca. 1981 unloading grain – Marge Uhrich

**Page 110**
City of Airdrie Emergency Services, Steve Scott and Tyler Sinclair – City of Airdrie; East Lake Recreation and Wellness Centre staff – City of Airdrie; Buzz Lorimer – Heloise Lorimer; Airdrie School class 1953 – Catherine (McIvor) Schafer

**Page 111**
Airdrie Emergency Services Candy Cane Run – Airdrie Emergency Services; Airdrie's own award winning yodeler Miriam Dreher – *Airdrie City View*; Baseball player James Medori – *Airdrie City View*; Airdrie "street kids" (!) ca. 1915, back row (L to R) Harold Soper, Vernon Flett, Albert Bailey, front row (L to R) Alberta Farr, Joe Jenkins, Jean Edwards, Cassie Jenkins – Heloise Lorimer; Airdrie July 1 Parade – City of Airdrie

**Page 112**
Dr. W. F. Edwards – Jean M. Edwards, Our Family History (Personal family history booklet printed ca. early 2000s); Group in front of drugstore identified as back row (L to R) Roy Edwards, Will Pole, Dr. Edwards and front row (L to R) Flo Thorburn, Anna Edwards, Nellie Pole – Jean M. Edwards, Our Family History (Personal family history booklet printed ca. early 2000s).

**Page 113**
Formula for 2 week old baby by Dr. W. F. Edwards – Nose Creek Valley Museum; Inside the drugstore – Elaine McCracken

**Page 114**
All photos – Heloise Lorimer

**Page 115**
Girls baseball team – Heloise Lorimer; Heloise Lorimer celebrating her 96th birthday – Anna Rebus; Airdrie Supply Store – Heloise Lorimer

**Page 116**
Ralph and Marilyn McCall – Marilyn McCall

**Page 117**
All photos – Marilyn McCall

**Page 118**
Brian Jackson close-up - Lucas Weigelt; Brian Jackson speaking – Neil Koven Photography

**Page 119**
Paul Brandt – Paul Brandt website www.paulbrandt.com/media.htm; Paul Brandt in Belize – Samaritan's Purse

**Page 120**
Linda Bruce – City of Airdrie

**Page 121**
Tim Harriman – Christa Boccabella

**Page 122**
Robin Burwash (1987) receiving Guy Weadick Memorial Trophy – Calgary Exhibition and Stampede Archives; Ron David (1987) – Calgary Exhibition and Stampede Archives

**Page 123**
Jim Dunn – Dunn family; Jim Nevada – Kathy Lind

**Page 125**
Airdrie water tower – City of Airdrie; Airdrie library – Marilyn McCall; Grain elevators – Nose Creek Valley Museum; Old Hotel – Anna Rebus

**Page 126**
Atlas Lumber Company 1912 – Heritage Park Historical Village, Calgary

**Page 127**
All historic photos – Heritage Park Historical Village, Calgary

**Page 128**
Old Hotel – Photographer unknown

**Page 129**
All photos – Anna Rebus

**Page 130**
Cummings Grain Company elevator – Glenbow Archives NA 1231-1

**Page 131**
Grain elevator with train in front – Marge Uhrich; Grain elevator being demolished – Marilyn McCall

**Page 132**
Airdrie cemetery – Anna Rebus

**Page 133**
Airdrie United Church – Airdrie United Church; Church sign – Larry Bilben

**Page 135**
The Airdrie Restaurant (The Handy Lunch) – McCracken family;
Airdrie street view ca. 1907-1909 – Glenbow Archives PA 3689-335

**Page 136**
Plane – Trevor McTavish

**Page 137**
De Havilland Tiger Moth spray plane with Frank Young watching from below – Gerry Stauffer, Calgary;
Frank Young 1958 – Gerry Stauffer, Calgary; ATCO factory at the Airdrie Airport ca. 1960s – Glenbow Archives 5713-15;
Planes in a row – Trevor McTavish

**Page 138**
Honey tin at Nose Creek Valley Museum – Anna Rebus; The Jolly Shopper – Heritage Park Historical Village, Calgary (The small one storey building in front of The Jolly Shopper is the Post Office, which later became the Information Centre.)

**Page 139**
Store cat and Johnnie Loveday (1956) – Janet Loveday Mason; Dry goods at Nose Creek Valley Museum – Anna Rebus

**Page 140**
Dusan Milutinovic – Milutinovic family; Dusan's Clothing Store – Marilyn McCall

**Page 141**
Water tower under construction – Nose Creek Valley Museum; Water tower – City of Airdrie

**Page 142**
Paul Rabel at the Town and Country Centre library (1978) – Dan McKinnon; Airdrie Library bottom left – Marilyn McCall; Airdrie Public Library – City of Airdrie; Airdrie Public Library – City of Airdrie

**Page 143**
Environmental Education Centre – City of Airdrie; Girl with recycling box – R.J. Hawkey Elementary School Tree Huggers 2008

**Page 144**
City Hall – City of Airdrie

**Page 145**
Bylaws available at The Alberta Heritage Digitization Project – Municipal Bylaws of Alberta www.ourfutureourpast.ca; Village of Airdrie Office late 1960s – Pat Bennett; Town of Airdrie Office 1974 by Bert Jasperse – Provincial Archives of Alberta GR1989.0516/30 #1

**Page 147**
R.J. Hawkey Elementary School sign – City of Airdrie; Street signs (Farr Cr, Jensen Dr, McCracken Cres) – Anna Rebus; Iron Horse Park – Iron Horse Park; Cooper's Crossing sign – WestMark Holdings Ltd; Bert Church High School sign – City of Airdrie; Ralph McCall sign – City of Airdrie

**Page 148**
A.E. Bowers and the Bowers Family – Nose Creek Valley Museum; Bert Church – Alexa Church

**Page 149**
Bowen family – Vera Bowen; George and Eleanor Cooper – Ann Hollands; Croxford family home and Thomas Croxford family – Nose Creek Valley Museum

**Page 150**
Roy and Lillian Edwards – Elaine McCracken; Bob Edwards – Opal Edwards; Les Farr and Muriel Van Sickle – Heloise Lorimer; Tom and Nancy Farr family – Heloise Lorimer; Lafe Van Sickle and Art Farr – Heloise Lorimer

**Page 151**
T. Flett Blacksmith Shop – Heritage Park Historical Village, Calgary; Ed Fletcher – Heloise Lorimer; Frank and Marianne Hawkey Family 1934 – Mary Underschultz; Annie and Robert Luther Hawkey – Marjorie (Hawkey) Lefevre

**Page 152**
R.J. Hawkey – R.J. Hawkey School; Iron Horse Park – Ray Gibbs; Knud Jensen – Lilly Jensen; Lilly Jensen – Lilly Jensen

**Page 153**
Lulu and Jim McCracken – Elaine McCracken; Martin McKee – Neil Koven Photography; Dick and Annie Morris and family – Olive Morris

**Page 154**
Muriel Clayton – Glenbow Archives NA 598-4; Ralph McCall – Marilyn McCall; Ted Lord – Dan McKinnon

**Page 155**
James Thorburn – City of Airdrie; Veterans – *Airdrie City View*

**Page 157**
Members of the Airdrie Horticultural Society at the Airdrie Community Gardens – Kim Sundset

**Page 158**
Cory Habberfield and his 4-H winning cow – Tami Hort; Heavy Horse at the Airdrie Canada Day Parade – Wendy Brownlee; Cooper's Crossing Parkland – Veronika Cindric

**Page 159**
Old Airdrie – Jane Romanishko; Airdrie Regional ARTS Society founders and board of directors – Kristen Shima Photography

**Page 160**
Bert Church Live Theatre stage – Kristy Reimer Photography; Ballet dancers – Nose Creek Valley Museum (*Airdrie Echo* archives); Airdrie Little Theatre – Robert D. Christie; Children on stage – City of Airdrie

**Page 161**
Airdrie Community Choir 1985-1986 – Eileen Silvertson; Piano keyboard – Anna Rebus; Airdrie Community Choir 2007-2008 – Kelly Warner

**Page 162**
Two men standing at cenotaph – *Airdrie City View*; Children looking at memorial wreaths – *Airdrie City View*; Members of the Ladies Auxiliary – Elaine McCracken; Veterans standing with flags – *Airdrie City View*

**Page 163**
Airdrie and District Rotary Club Soap Box Derby – City of Airdrie; Airdrie and District Rotary Club – Airdrie and District Rotary Club; Kinsmen Club of Airdrie – Kinsmen Club of Airdrie

**Page 164**
Over 50 Club members dancing and on bus tour – Over 50 Club; Members of the Over 50 Club choir – Jan Bowhay; Wild Rose Shriners Club – Hugh Hamilton; Shriners on horseback in the Airdrie July 1 parade – City of Airdrie

**Page 165**
Executive of the Nose Creek Historical Society – Sharon Bilben; Airdrie Chamber of Commerce – Airdrie Chamber of Commerce

**Page 166**
Airdrie Girl Guides all photos – Twyla Jenkins; Airdrie Scouts on the ice – Larry Bilben; Airdrie Scouts Kub Kar Rally – Ken Rozniak

**Page 167**
4-H club members viewing livestock – Dan McKinnon; Members of the Airdrie Helping Hands 4-H Multi Club at a public speaking event February 2008 – Christine Jorstad; Marjorie Clayton – Dan McKinnon

**Page 168**
All photos for Airdrie Horticultural Society – Kim Sundset

**Page 169**
Airdrie and District Agricultural Society – Airdrie and District Agricultural Society

**Page 170**
Airdrie Lioness Club at July 1 Parade – Airdrie Lioness Club; Airdrie Lions Club 1971 – Lorna Hunt; Joyce Lewis with pie – Elaine McCracken; Airdrie Lions Club 2005 – Airdrie Lions Club

**Page 171**
Airdrie Rodeo Ranch Association – *Airdrie City View*

**Page 172**
Boy in goal – Lilly Jensen; Airdrie girls drill practice 1928 – Heloise Lorimer

**Page 173**

Airdrie Oldtimers hockey team – Heloise Lorimer; Airdrie's ice hockey team 1928-1929 – Heloise Lorimer; Airdrie's ice hockey team mid 1930s – Heloise Lorimer; Airdrie Lightning player – *Airdrie City View*; Airdrie Thunder player – *Airdrie City View*

**Page 174**

Baseball player sliding into a base – *Airdrie City View*; Airdrie Little League team – Airdrie Little League, Rob Morphew; Airdrie's baseball team 1928 – Heloise Lorimer; Airdrie's baseball team date unknown – Heloise Lorimer

**Page 175**

Women curling 2008 – Larry Bilben; Curlers Tom Farr, Wilfred Clapperton, Ernie DeWitt and Walter Moen at the Golden Jubilee Bonspiel in Calgary, 1954 – Glenbow Archives NA 5600-7330b

**Page 176**

Figure skater – *Airdrie City View*; Ballet dancers – Peter Carlton Photography; Swimmers about to race – Airdrie Swim Club; Gymnast Julie Warnock – Photo by Grace Chiu/GraceClick; Swimmer Joel Greenshields – *Airdrie City View*; BMX racer Samantha Cools – *Airdrie City View*

**Page 177**

Airdrie Storm Football players – City of Airdrie; Soccer players – *Airdrie City View*;
Bert Church High School Chargers (football) – *Airdrie City View*; Young soccer players – Larry Bilben; Bert Church High School Chargers (basketball), Dominyc Coward – *Airdrie City View*

**PHOTO CREDITS PART THREE: OPPORTUNITY FOR THE FUTURE**

**Page 179**
(Opportunity for the future)
Children playing near water in Waterstone (L to R) Quinn Richards, Skylar Sawatzky and Matthew Sawatzky – City of Airdrie

**Page 181**
The Van Sickle's first car (1927) – Heloise Lorimer; Family walking down the street – City of Airdrie

**Page 182**
Airdrie Hardware Store – Nose Creek Valley Museum; Modern stores – City of Airdrie; Drawings – Logan Berreth

**Page 183**
Airdrie Tower – Christian Lowry; all other drawings – Logan Berreth

**Page 184**
Mr. Hallman's team of Hackney horses – Heloise Lorimer; City of Airdrie Smart Car – City of Airdrie; Cyclists – Cooper's Crossing/WestMark Holdings Ltd

## Page 185
People helping out around the city – City of Airdrie

## Page 186
Airdrie street view in front of W. Stuart Lumber and Coal shop (ca. 1912) – Glenbow Archives NA 2547-10; Artist's rendering of new development on Main Street – City of Airdrie; View of Main Street – City of Airdrie

## Page 187
McKee Business Centre and hanging baskets – City of Airdrie, Genesis Place - WestMark Holdings Ltd

## Page 188
Airdrie street view (ca. 1914-1917) – Glenbow Archives 1222-1

## Page 189
Airdrie street view, 2008 – Larry Bilben.


# PHOTO CREDITS – TIMELINE/ABOUT THE AUTHOR/NOTES

## Page 192
Airdrie railway station 1904 – Heloise Lorimer; Anvil at Nose Creek Valley Museum – Anna Rebus; Dr. W. F. Edwards – Jean M. Edwards, Our Family History (Personal family history booklet printed ca. early 2000s); T. Vincent – City of Airdrie; A.E. Bowers – City of Airdrie; Leslie Farr – City of Airdrie; Influenza epidemic poster – Glenbow Archives NA 4548-5; Lloyd Flett – Glenbow Archives NA 2466-1

## Page 193
Joseph J. Stewart – Elaine McCracken; Airdrie United Church – Airdrie United Church; J.R. McCracken – Elaine McCracken; James Thorburn – City of Airdrie; William R. Jenkins – City of Airdrie; Lafayette Van Sickle – City of Airdrie; Alberta Wheat Pool grain elevators – Nose Creek Valley Museum (Airdrie Echo archives); Inez Clayton – Roberta Whittaker; R.J. Hawkey – City of Alrdrie

## Page 194
Nat Clogg – City of Airdrie; Sim Meyer – City of Airdrie; Knud Jensen – Lilly Jensen; Water tower under construction – Nose Creek Valley Museum; John Loveday – City of Airdrie; Robert T. Edwards – Elaine McCracken; Walter Moen – Elaine McCracken; Darrell Bennett – City of Airdrie

## Page 195
Children on stage at Bert Church Live Theatre – City of Airdrie; Ron Davidson – City of Airdrie; Dayliner train – Provincial Archives of Alberta PR1998.0880/0037; Snowdrift – Marilyn McCall, Stephanie Harris – Harris family; Grant McLean – City of Airdrie; Rick Hansen – Alan Tennant; Olympic Torch – Loreen Hamilton

**Page 196**

Dan Oneil – City of Airdrie; Stamp from Japan – Bilben family; Airdrie Festival of Lights – City of Airdrie; South Korean totem pole at Nose Creek Park – City of Airdrie; Environmental Education Centre – City of Airdrie; Linda Bruce – City of Airdrie East Lake Recreation and Wellness Centre – City of Airdrie

**Page 200**

About the author, Anna Rebus – Kristy Reimer Photography/AirdrieLIFE Magazine

**Page 236**

Aileen Van Sickle in her "automobile" ready for a ride – Heloise Lorimer

**Page 237**

Getting ready to till the garden – Lilly Jensen

**Page 238**

Going for a pony ride – Lilly Jensen

**Page 239**

Family on the Howe farm – Thomas Howe

*index*

# Index

## Symbols

*notes*

*notes*

# notes

# notes